Britain and the French Revolution

Pearson
Education

SEMINAR STUDIES IN HISTORY

Britain and the French Revolution

CLIVE EMSLEY

An imprint of Pearson Education
Harlow, England · London · New York · Reading, Massachusetts · San Francisco · Toronto · Don Mills, Ontario · Sydney
Tokyo · Singapore · Hong Kong · Seoul · Taipei · Cape Town · Madrid · Mexico City · Amsterdam · Munich · Paris · Milan

Pearson Education Limited
Edinburgh Gate
Harlow
Essex CM20 2JE
England
and Associated Companies throughout the world.

Visit us on the World Wide Web at:
www.pearsoneduc.com

First published 2000

ISBN 0-582-36961-4 PPR

British Library Cataloguing-in-Publication Data
A catalogue record for this book is available from the British Library

Library of Congress Cataloging-in-Publication Data
Emsley, Clive
Britain and the French Revolution/Clive Emsley
p. cm. -- (Seminar studies in history)
Includes bibliographical references (p.) and index
ISBN 0-582-36961-4
1. Great Britain--Politics and government--1789-1820. 2. France--History--Revolution 1789-1799--Foreign public opinion, British. 3. France--History--Revolution, 1789-1799--Influence. 4. Great Britain--Civilization--French influences. 5. Great Britain--Foreign relations--1789-1820. 6. Great Britain-- Foreign relations--France. 7. France--Foreign relations--Great Britain. 8. Public opinion--Great Britain--History 9. France--Foreign relations--1789-1815. I. Title. II. Series.
DA520.E47 2000
941.07′3--dc21 00-026029

Set by 7 in 10/12 Sabon Roman
Printed in Malaysia LSP

CONTENTS

AN INTRODUCTION TO THE SERIES

Such is the pace of historical enquiry in the modern world that there is an ever-widening gap between the specialist article or monograph, incorporating the results of current research, and general surveys, which inevitably become out of date. *Seminar Studies in History* are designed to bridge this gap. The series was founded by Patrick Richardson in 1966 and his aim was to cover major themes in British, European and World history. Between 1980 and 1996 Roger Lockyer continued his work, before handing the editorship over to Clive Emsley and Gordon Martel. Clive Emsley is Professor of History at the Open University, while Gordon Martel is Professor of International History at the University of Northern British Columbia, Canada and Senior Research Fellow at De Montfort University.

All the books are written by experts in their field who are not only familiar with the latest research but have often contributed to it. They are frequently revised, in order to take account of new information and interpretations. They provide a selection of documents to illustrate major themes and provoke discussion, and also a guide to further reading. The aim of *Seminar Studies* is to clarify complex issues without over-simplifying them, and to stimulate readers into deepening their knowledge and understanding of major themes and topics.

NOTE ON REFERENCING SYSTEM

Readers should note that numbers in square brackets [5] refer them to the corresponding entry in the Bibliography at the end of the book (specific page numbers are given in italics). A number in square brackets preceded by *Doc.* [*Doc.* 5] refers readers to the corresponding item in the Documents section which follows the main text.

ACKNOWLEDGEMENTS

The publishers are grateful to the following for permission to use copyright material:

The British Library for permission to use *The Zenith of French Glory* and *Presages of the Millenium*, caricatures by James Gillray.

PART ONE INTRODUCTION

CHAPTER ONE

ISSUES AND HISTORIOGRAPHY

Historians argue over the causes, the course, and the consequences of the French Revolution. They differ about the dates of its beginning and its end. Yet few, if any, would deny that it had profound effects far beyond the frontiers of France. Some of the effects are relatively easy to pinpoint and provoke little debate; but there can also be significant differences of opinion, especially when historians move away from a detailed chronology of events to assessing the broader patterns and meanings of those events. Thus, while a chronicle of the impact of the French Revolution on Britain is relatively straightforward, what that impact meant in the broader picture of political and social change, of social development and class relations, of national self-consciousness remains a matter of dispute.

The period from 1688 to 1815 was one of intense rivalry between Britain and France, sometimes described as the 'second hundred years war'. The two states clashed in the four corners of the world over markets and imperial possessions. Since the reign of Louis XIV, France, a dominant continental power, had appeared to successive British governments to be aiming at European hegemony; and this was something which they could never countenance. Britain's wars against the French Revolution and, subsequently, against Napoleon, provided the climax to this facet of the rivalry and they settled the matter in Britain's favour.

But it was not only in matters of French hegemony in Europe, of markets and imperial possessions that the two countries were rivals. Eighteenth-century France was Catholic. She was ruled by a monarchy which aspired to absolutism, and this aspiration provided the model for most other princes of continental Europe. The British were fiercely Protestant and proud of the liberties and the balanced constitution which they considered they had won by the Glorious Revolution of 1688–89. They believed that these liberties and their constitution were examples for their less fortunate continental neighbours. Indeed, some eighteenth-century French thinkers pointed to what they understood to be Britain's 'balanced constitution' of the king in parliament with the counterweights of lords and commons, to the separation of executive, legislative and judicial powers, and they suggested that such structures might benefit their own country. At the same time there were Britons who, particularly from the 1780s, looked to changing French models which, they believed, might be taken up and usefully developed for their own national context [27]. Again, the revolutionary and Napoleonic wars appeared to settle the matter in favour of constitutional monarchies and parliamentary structures, though the extent to which Britain can be considered as a model remains a moot point.

Changing political, economic and social contexts foster changes in historical perceptions and interpretations. During the nineteenth century the Anglo-French conflict of 1793–1815 was described as 'the Great War'; and then a new, catastrophic conflict in Europe, meant that the term was no longer applicable. During the Second World War and in its aftermath, however, patriotic parallels could be found by some historians who described the earlier conflict in terms of a gallant Britain standing alone against a hostile ideology – Jacobinism – and dictator – Napoleon, even Robespierre – who dominated continental Europe by force of arms [11; 12]. The patriotic parallels drawn by Arthur Bryant and others would find favour with few contemporary academic historians; and more recently the wars have been studied as a way into understanding the development of class and/or national consciousness [18; 124; 126].

The sons of the Whig grandees, so long out of power under George III, published the papers of their forebears in the early nineteenth century with commentaries which portrayed the Whigs as 'friends of the people', long-standing supporters of parliamentary reform, who were denied power by 'old corruption' and a blinkered monarch. A similar interpretation was put forward by non-patrician radicals and reformers who maintained that some 40 years of political reaction had begun in Britain during the early 1790s, and had continued until the passage of the Great Reform Bill in 1832. A broadly Whig interpretation subsequently suited those historians, like J.L. and Barbara Hammond and Sidney and Beatrice Webb, who, at the beginning of the twentieth century, sketched out the history of the continuing struggle for parliamentary reform and for the recognition of trades unions [24; 25; 26]. The French Revolution is central to the Whig interpretation since it appeared to have provided the opportunity for a reactionary Toryism to tar all reform with the brush of revolution and thus to persecute and suppress those calling both for political reform and the right to organise and campaign against the low wages and bad conditions of the early stages of the industrial revolution. At the same time the Whig interpretation, by implication at least, suggests first, that British reformers and radicals had political arguments intellectually superior to those of their persecutors, and secondly, that they were moderate and constitutional with only a few eccentric hotheads seeking violent, revolutionary change.

While, eventually, there was parliamentary reform – with the Great Reform Act of 1832 being passed by a ministry led by Earl Grey who, as Charles Grey, had been a leading figure among the young Foxite Whig activists of the 1790s – it is by no means agreed that the radicals and reformers won the political debates at the time of the French Revolution. The loyalists put cogent, well-made arguments and did not necessarily defeat their opponents simply with repression and what passes as the English 'reign of terror' [35; 94]. Moreover the demands for reform went far wider than the call for changes in the ways that parliament was elected and constituencies were spread and structured. The wars against revolutionary and Napoleonic France were extremely costly in men and money. The financial costs were met by the efficiency of what John Brewer has described as the Hanoverian 'military-fiscal state' [121], but the scale of those costs drew attention to the peculation and greed of politicians and officials who ran the system often for their own financial benefit. Demands for reform of this system came from men who, like William Wilberforce, could normally be called upon as loyalists to support the government, and the end of the war witnessed a steady dismantling of the Hanoverian war machine by men who were not political radicals [47; 128].

While almost all demands for change could be, and often were, branded 'revolutionary' in Britain during the 1790s, aspirations for reform were not confined solely to Foxite Whigs, political radicals or revolutionaries. The question of whether revolutions are the work of individuals who seek violent political change, or processes which gather momentum from the failure of one group to maintain power and then work themselves out in the resulting conflict between different groups who aspire to seize that power, is not one that can be explored at length here. However, recent research into attitudes among a cross-section of British reformers and radicals during the decade of the French Revolution suggests an ambivalence towards violence, even among some of the most respectable. A comparison between the *sans-culottes* of revolutionary Paris and the artisans who joined British corresponding societies has drawn attention to considerable similarities [84]; and if debate on the significance of a revolutionary underground, and on the potential for revolution in Britain during the period is not yet resolved, it is clear that radicalism was by no means always as moderate and constitutionally minded as the Whig interpretation suggested [13; 30; 80; 82; 97; 99].

What follows is a broad survey of the impact of the French Revolution on Britain. The book is organised thematically. It begins with a general survey of the ideological debate sparked off by the Revolution. It moves from there to explore the Revolution's effects on parliamentary politics at Westminster, on the development of reform, radicalism, and loyalism and, in Ireland, on the origins and course of rebellion. From here the focus shifts to the causes and impact of the war against revolutionary France; and this is followed by a discussion of the recurrent, serious food shortages during the decade. The concluding chapter offers some overall assessments.

PART TWO ANALYSIS

CHAPTER TWO

IDEAS

The upheavals which constituted the opening stages of the French Revolution coincided with centenary celebrations in Britain for the Glorious Revolution of 1688. To many it appeared that the French were now taking steps to reject absolutism and to establish both the kind of constitutional monarchy and the forms of personal 'liberty' which freeborn Englishmen had boasted as their birthright since the exile of the Stuart dynasty. Such perceptions were particularly appealing to political radicals and those of a liberal political inclination. For the young William Wordsworth it was 'bliss' to be alive; the MP Samuel Romilly 'rejoiced', perceived a 'very sincere and general joy' in Britain, and looked forward to 'the important consequences which must follow throughout Europe' [quoted in 4 *pp. 39–40*]. Among such liberal-minded individuals, especially Protestant Dissenters, there were those who considered that, good as the English system might appear, there were still abuses which needed to be ironed out. Dissenters and Catholics were debarred from political life, though it was possible for the former at least to take office by becoming 'occasional conformists', that is taking holy communion once a year in the established church. There had been applications to parliament by, and on behalf of, Protestant dissenters to repeal these Acts in March 1787 and May 1789; a third approach was made in March 1790. And while the agitation for parliamentary reform had subsided with the decline of the Association Movement of 1780 (see below p. 22), the reformist literature remained in circulation and reformist aspirations were still to be met.

BURKE AND PAINE

It was against this background that, on 4 November 1789, Dr Richard Price, a dissenting minister well-known for his works on political economy and population, preached a sermon 'On the Love of our Country' to the Society for Commemorating the Revolution of 1688. Price stressed that the Revolution of 1688 had been based on three principles: liberty of conscience; the right to resist power when abused; and the right to choose and reject rulers. However, he believed that the business of 1688 had been left unfinished, and he went on to urge the abolition of the Test and Corporation Acts, which restricted the first of these principles, and a reform of the system of representation in parliament which was currently leading to 'government by corruption'. The events in France, following closely on the American Revolution, he believed, were the heralds of change across the world [*Doc. 1*]. It was this sermon which prompted Edmund Burke to write his powerful *Reflections on the Revolution in France* [1; *Doc. 2*].

Born in Dublin in 1729, the son of an Irish barrister, Edmund Burke had himself studied law. He entered parliament as an MP at the end of 1765; from then until the early 1780s he acted as a powerful spokesman for the Whigs in parliament. He had denounced misgovernment in the American colonies and was opposed to fighting the colonists in their war of independence. He had denounced the exploitation of India by the East India Company and had taken a leading role in launching the impeachment of Warren Hastings, the former Governor General of Bengal and, subsequently, of British India. He was sympathetic to religious toleration. But by the end of the 1780s Burke had become disillusioned with the Whig party, not least because of the stance taken by its leaders, notably Fox, during the Regency Crisis of 1788–89. He had supported 'economical reform', which he understood essentially as the removal of secret influence and corruption in government, but he always had his doubts about political reform. Suggestions that Britain might take a cue from events in France and embark on a series of constitutional changes, including parliamentary reform, incensed him. It seems too that he saw in the crowd action in Paris an echo of the Gordon Riots which had terrorised London in 1780, and thus, rather than an example to follow, France was providing a serious warning for Britain of things to avoid [43]. 'France', he proclaimed, 'has brought undisguised calamities at a higher price than any nation has purchased the most unequivocal blessings! France has bought poverty by crime!' In sum, her example was 'an irreparable calamity … to mankind' (Burke, *Reflections*, Everyman Edition, pp. 35 and 36).

Initially there were few who shared Burke's fears, or at least few who were prepared to make any such concerns public. The *Reflections* prompted many critical replies. Perhaps the most astute and cogent was *Vindiciae Gallicae*, written by James Mackintosh, a young, unsuccessful Scottish doctor, who would soon change his profession and make a career as a successful lawyer and a liberal politician. Quite simply, Mackintosh explained, Burke had got it wrong. It was mistaken to imply any excellence to the old institutions of France; these had been inimicable to liberty. Drawing on the ideas of their ancestors and the experience of other countries, the French had every right to contemplate the general principles which regulated society and to reform their institutions accordingly. The validity of their actions should depend only upon subsequent approval. But while intellectually sound and highly regarded, especially among the Whigs, *Vindiciae Gallicae* was not written in a way that made it readily accessible to all readers. Tom Paine's *The Rights of Man* [7; *Doc. 3*] was quite different and it rapidly became the most popular and influential response to Burke.

Paine had been born in Norfolk in 1737. He began life following his father's trade of staymaker; later he became an excise man, but was dismissed for writing a pamphlet demanding better pay. In 1774 he crossed to America where he played an influential role as a pamphleteer on the side of the colonists in the run up to and during the war of independence. He journeyed to France in 1787, crossing to England to promote an iron bridge which he had designed. *Part One* of *The Rights of Man* appeared in March 1791, and even before the appearance of *Part Two* early in the following year, the ideological debate had begun to polarise around the writings of Burke and Paine.

Burke's *Reflections* remains one of the most powerful statements in favour of political conservatism, yet he always saw himself as defending Whig principles, the constitutional monarchy, and the parliamentary system based on checks and balances. The Glorious Revolution of 1688, as interpreted by Burke, did not introduce new principles; it changed the monarch, but kept the principle of heredity. It was merely another reformation in a tradition, begun with the Magna Carta, of preserving constitutional inheritance and freedoms. In Burke's estimation, the best societies and political structures were organic; they grew and matured over centuries, constantly evolving and adapting themselves to the present. Political societies were partnerships between the dead, the living, and the as yet unborn, and the best arrangements were conventions sanctified by custom and tradition. Equality and abstract rights were chimeras; the much vaunted 'reason' of French philosophers was dangerous; and it was sheer folly, as the French were doing, to seek to rewrite constitutions from scratch on the basis of theory. Paine, in contrast, was not a great constitutional thinker but rather a populist with a racy style and a ready wit. He was also a republican. He urged that men had the right to decide for themselves on their form of government; this was not something that could be set by one generation for its successors, and there was no justification for heredity in any part of government. In the second part of his pamphlet he outlined plans for a root and branch reform in Britain, even advocating new forms of taxation and welfare provision [34].

The clash between Burke and Paine has come to crystallise the political argument which developed in Britain in the wake of the French Revolution. The argument was conducted at its primary level in pamphlet literature, but the ideas spread to a much wider audience through a variety of forms of media. Some of the pamphlets were edited and republished in popular cheap editions. In January 1792 in Sheffield, for example, there were 1,400 subscribers to a sixpenny (2½p) edition of *Part One* of *The Rights of Man*. The pamphlet debate was a reflection of the vibrant print culture of eighteenth-century Britain, of the spread of newspaper readership, and of the increasing importance of the press in politics. Newspapers themselves took sides in the arguments about reform and the events in France, and the audience of eighteenth-century newspapers went far beyond the individual purchasers of single copies. Purchased copies were commonly passed on from hand to hand to other readers. They were available in clubs and taverns, and could be read in print-shop windows; at each of these venues they were read aloud and discussed aloud. There were also broadsheets and ballads printed to announce or to comment upon particular events, such as the execution of Louis XVI. The caricatures published by men like Isaac Cruikshank, James Gillray and Thomas Rowlandson also commented upon current events and, like newspapers, could be viewed and discussed when displayed in print-shop windows. Political activists and sharp-eyed entrepreneurs developed other kinds of iconography as a kind of shorthand for the ideas and arguments. The images of a Cruikshank or a Gillray were reproduced on beakers, jugs, mugs, kerchiefs, medallions and tokens; Rowlandson's caricature *The Contrast*, which set the 'Religion, morality, loyalty, obedience to the laws, independence, personal security, justice, inheritance, protection of property, industry, national prosperity, happiness' of 'British Liberty' against the 'Atheism, perjury, rebellion, treason, anarchy, murder, equality, madness, cruelty, injustice, treachery, ingratitude, idleness, famine, national and private ruin, misery' of the French equivalent, appeared on a mug as well as at the head of a loyalist broadsheet ballad, *The New Hearts of Oak*. Radicals made great play with Burke's unfortunate reference to 'the swinish multitude' in the *Reflections*, and made the pig an ironic emblem for the people. Loyalists played on the traditions of national stereotypes which celebrated the bluff, hearty Englishman and denigrated the scrawny, poverty-stricken Frenchman; they also milked every ounce of sentimentality from images of Louis XVI's farewell to his family and every ounce of horror from revolutionary violence [147].

While, in the *Reflections,* Burke warned about the dangers and violence inherent in the Revolution and, in response, Paine jeered that he 'pities the plumage and forgets the dying bird', the primary intellectual arguments of the 1790s did not focus simply on the events of the Revolution and the extent to which the French people were justified in changing their constitutional structures. Questions were also posed about the nature of government in general. Did people have the right to resist their rulers? How had civil society first been established? Was it a contract between free individuals who exchanged natural rights for civil rights? Was it a contract between governors and governed, in which the only rights that ever existed were those granted by society? Participants in the debates returned to, and built upon, texts from the constitutional conflicts of the seventeenth century. Liberals and radicals justified their claims for reform by appeals to, in particular, James Harrington and John Locke, who had commented upon and analysed, respectively, the constitutional upheavals of the 1640s and 1650s and the Revolution of 1688. Some looked back even further to a mythical Saxon golden age destroyed by conquest and the imposition of the 'Norman yoke'. They were also men of the Enlightenment who saw human beings as rational creatures, and creatures who had to be permitted to use their reason to change the unreasonable and hasten the perfectibility of society. Their conservative opponents, in contrast, urged that there was far more to human beings than simply their reason. Surely there were other facets of human nature that were significant to their actions and beliefs? Were not human beings as much creatures of passion as of reason? Were they not influenced by the climate and the social conditions in which they lived? And how could individuals be equal in property and rank when, manifestly, they were so unequal in strength of body and mind, and in terms of age and sex?

The debates were not infused with the same degree of religious fervour as many in the seventeenth century, yet the role of a supreme being or of a providential God figured prominently on both sides of the arguments. Religion remained a significant force in eighteenth-century Britain and, as J.C.D. Clark has been at pains to emphasise, Britain's old regime remained at least formally a confessional state [15]. For some of the radicals, God was relegated to a prime mover. But for others, and for the conservatives, He remained active in human affairs. The magnitude of the upheaval in France, and subsequently the war and food shortages, excited elements of millenarianism. It appeared that the last days, as foretold in the Book of Revelation, were approaching. William Blake's paintings, such as *Albion*, his 'prophesies' *America* and *Europe*, and his poetic fragment, *The French Revolution*, while not always easily interpreted, provide some of the most striking examples of such millenarianism among one of the most radical artists of the day [152; 154]. And both radical and conservative camps contained those who understood the events heralded by the French Revolution as divine punishment and a warning of the need for a reformation of morals.

RADICAL VARIATIONS

While the debates of the 1790s were sparked by the Revolution, they never became confined to arguments over the rights and wrongs of the event. As the Revolution moved on into war and terror, the intellectual ferment in Britain also moved on. Events in France, and then the war, continued to occupy some polemicists, but others, especially on the radical side, moved on to consider the future of society, the treatment of the poor, the rights of women, and to provide a rich legacy for the future.

Paine's own political polemics did not end with the *Rights of Man* and his departure for France in September 1792, just ahead of his conviction, *in absentia*, for seditious libel and a sentence of outlawry. While in France he wrote *The Age of Reason*, in which he outlined his creed as a Deist and condemned Christianity as a dangerous irrelevance whose textual authority, the Bible, was a compound of contradictory fables. The book was soon available in England where the radicals of the London Corresponding Society (hereafter LCS, and see below p. 30) sponsored a cheap edition, for which the publisher was prosecuted, and where Richard Watson, Bishop of Llandaff, replied with a rather ineffectual *Apology for the Bible*. In 1797 Paine published *Agrarian Justice* in which, to solve the problem of poverty, he argued that landowners be required to pay into a national fund that could be used to provide first, a £15 bounty for every 21 year-old with which to start out in the world, and second, a £10 annual pension for everyone aged 50 and over.

Similar agrarian ideas were already being developed by Thomas Spence, an idiosyncratic Newcastle schoolmaster who had moved to London, probably in 1788, to eke out a precarious living as bookseller and writer on economic and social matters. Caught up with the excitement of the French Revolution and the growth of radical politics, Spence sold Paine's work alongside his own and, at different times, he was committed to prison for selling both. But Spence was critical of Paine's *Agrarian Justice* for not going back to the root cause of society's problems which, he considered, lay in the ownership of land and the power that derived from this. Any tax on landowners would merely cement the established system. Just as Paine had argued that one generation could not impose a political system on its successors, so Spence argued that no generation could impose a private distribution of landed property on its successors. There should be a universal right to landed property; it should be held in common by the population of the parish since the open access to land would guarantee employment and ensure fair and adequate wages. By permitting a few extremist members of the LCS to train with weapons on his premises in 1794, and even more by his 1795 pamphlet *The End of Oppression: or, a Quartern Loaf for Two-pence*, Spence showed that he was not averse to the use of physical force to achieve these ends [*Doc. 22*]. He does not appear to have been much involved with the revolutionary United Englishmen of the late 1790s, but by the turn of the century organised groups of Spenceans were to be found in the radical milieu. And if the violent element among the

Spenceans disappeared at the end of the Regency, Spence's agrarian ideas fed into both Owenite radicalism and Chartism [5; 32].

John Thelwall was more genteel and probably less extreme than Spence, but he was equally suspect in the eyes of the authorities for his membership of the LCS, for his radical, and at times intemperate and violent, lectures, and for publicly glorying in the name of a *sans-culotte*. He was not a particularly original thinker, and much of his rhetoric centred on the rights of the people to discuss politics and to censure the behaviour of government, particularly with reference to the war and its expense. Nevertheless, Thelwall began to develop a radical version of natural rights theory moving in the same direction as some of Paine's ideas. In Thelwall's eyes society had a duty to help individuals and to ensure to the poor as a matter of natural right the redistribution of a surplus of historically produced labour. He also never ceased to praise the principles of the French Revolution in particular for emphasising that men had natural rights, that abuses did not become virtues because of their antiquity, and that the promotion of the happiness of humankind was the object of society [3; 37].

Thelwall was one of the radicals who stood with one foot among the radical artisans of the LCS and the other among the more well-to-do, intellectual grouping of generally young men, who were equally inspired by the Revolution. This group included the poets Wordsworth and Coleridge, and also the political thinker William Godwin [148; 155]. The son of a dissenting minister, Godwin had himself begun his adult life as a minister. When the Revolution erupted, however, he was little concerned with religious matters, having moved to London during the 1780s and embarked on a literary career. The French Revolution inspired him to develop his ideas for the perfectibility of humankind. *The Enquiry Concerning the Principle of Political Justice and its Influence on General Virtue and Happiness* was begun in 1791 and published in two volumes in February 1793. Unlike most other political radicals, Godwin rejected the idea of natural rights. He saw the future perfectibility of humanity as emerging through the operation of what he called 'universal benevolence'. This was a moral obligation which, Godwin believed, rested on all men. No one had the right to dispose of his talents or wealth simply for his personal advantage or profit; and no one had the right to exercise power over anyone else. He was highly critical of the existing institutions of government, law and church, but he believed that these would wither away once universal benevolence began to function as it should. Godwin's criticisms were unsparing, but he escaped prosecution allegedly because, as Pitt is reported to have said, a book costing three guineas would be of little interest to radical artisans who could barely find three shillings. Probably the authorities also suspected that the complex, metaphysical arguments of

Political Justice would create difficulties of understanding for radical artisans. Nevertheless there is evidence that the book was known among such audiences. Its greatest impact, however, was on the Romantic poets and among similar intellectual circles in the early nineteenth century.

Godwin's personal creed led him to oppose marriage, yet in 1797 he married his pregnant mistress, Mary Wollstonecraft. She shared Godwin's disapproval of marriage and had already borne an illegitimate daughter to an American gentleman with whom she had lived while in France. More significantly, she had herself engaged in the political debate sparked by the French Revolution and had taken up the cause of women's rights. At the end of 1790 she had hurriedly written *A Vindication of the Rights of Men*, an attack on Burke and a denunciation of the existing state of English society. This followed the fairly traditional line of defending the actions of the French against Burke's condemnation. However in 1792 she published *A Vindication of the Rights of Woman*, a pamphlet which was to become a key document in the feminist canon in Britain, Europe and the United States. The title echoed that of Paine, and within the book Wollstonecraft stated that women should be represented in legislatures, equating their position with that of the unrepresented working men 'who pay for the support of royalty when they can scarcely stop their children's mouths with bread'. But her principle concern was education. Women and men were equally human and rational, yet women were kept in ignorance. Equal opportunities for all to acquire both information and rational skills would benefit all of humanity, destroying ignorance and oppressive government, and fostering the perfectibility of human nature [*Doc. 5*].

Wollstonecraft's feminist voice was relatively isolated, and in many respects it remained limited. Radical men in general had a masculine concept of citizenship; they commonly associated corruption and decadence with femininity, and they also tended to equate reason with masculinity and irrationality with femininity [14]. At the same time, both Wollstonecraft and the like-minded Mary Hays saw maternity and domestic concerns as women's duty and principal concerns; and it was much the same with those other women who participated in the debate on the Revolution and the subsequent war. While women seem to have engaged publicly in the political controversies of the 1790s to a much greater extent than ever before, their texts focused on education, morality, and religion – subjects considered as more 'acceptable' for women. Anna Laeticia Barbauld, for example, the wife of a Presbyterian minister, wrote powerfully against the barriers which inhibited the political participation of Dissenters, and she was highly critical of the war and the fast days decreed for the sake of British success. Barbauld's style and thinking were in a fairly traditional mould of reformist criticism, morality, and religion, and shared none of Wollstonecraft's precocious feminism. Yet, in many respects, the writings of

Barbauld and Wollstonecraft were symptomatic of the different directions taken by the reformist and radical thought sparked by the Revolution.

LOYALIST RESPONSES

As radical ideas diverged in different directions, so conservatives and loyalists continued to confront them. But much conservative and loyalist literature concentrated on the folly of the French and on the necessity of the war against them. Burke himself became more and more focused on the need to extirpate French principles. In August 1791 he published *An Appeal from the New to the Old Whigs*. He refuted the charge of political inconsistency levelled at him by former political allies and reiterated his belief that the theoretical principles which underpinned the activities of French revolutionaries were quite different from those which had inspired action in England a century before. Basing political structures on abstract notions of rights and the will of an untutored majority without any reference to duties and morality was, he reiterated, foolish in the extreme. Moreover, the line taken by his former colleagues would, he feared, lead to the dissemination in Britain of the dangerous principles of the French. When war came in early 1793 Burke saw it as a new kind of conflict and, in the four *Letters on a Regicide Peace*, penned between 1795 and 1797 and which constitute his last great political pamphlet, he warned against 'a Sansculottick peace', which would leave Jacobinism alive and a continuing threat to humanity.

While radical authors condemned the war as the sport of despots and the cause of food shortages, and while liberal reformers, styling themselves 'the Friends of Peace' (see below p. 34) condemned all war, and that against France particularly for being the cause of crippling taxation, a string of conservative polemicists followed Burke's lead on the conflict. John Bowles, for example, wrote a succession of pamphlets justifying the war and warning against any premature peace and concession to Jacobinism. Bowles was a barrister and an active magistrate in Surrey. He began to receive treasury money for writing conservative propaganda in 1792, the year in which he published *A Protest against Thomas Paine's 'Rights of Man'*; by the middle of the 1790s he had a string of lucrative government offices which enabled him to give up his legal career and devote a considerable amount of time to pamphleteering. Like several others, Bowles was not a mere slavish follower of Burke, but rather a kindred spirit. He had a sincere personal faith in the excellence of the English constitution which he regarded as under threat from French principles. He also saw the Revolution as a vast conspiracy directed against the established civil, political and religious institutions of Europe [94; 131]. This conspiracy theory of the Revolution found its first forceful statement in an essay by a

French *émigré* priest, Augustin de Barruel, *Mémoires pour servir à l'histoire du jacobinisme* (1797), and then, in the same year, in a pamphlet by John Robison, Professor of Natural Law at the University of Edinburgh, *Proofs of a Conspiracy against All the Religions and Governments of Europe carried on in the Secret Meetings of Free Masons, Illuminati, and Reading Societies*.

Bowles and Robison were among the contributors to the *Anti-Jacobin Review*, a monthly journal which began in July 1798 as an organ of loyal and conservative propaganda; it continued until 1821. The *Review* was the direct successor to the *Anti-Jacobin, or Weekly Political Examiner* which, for just under a year, had set out to refute what it considered to be the dangerous doctrines of sedition being fervently circulated in the country by British 'Jacobins'. Both the weekly and the monthly benefited from ministerial involvement and patronage, but government involvement with the press was nothing new. In the early years of the French Revolution Pitt's government was subsidising parts of the press to the tune of £5,000 a year. From October 1792 it fostered a new newspaper, the daily *Sun*; and from January 1793 it financed the daily *True Briton*. Both of these papers were edited by the subsidised treasury author, John Heriot. At roughly the same time the government appears to have been involved with the creation of the Anglican periodical, the *British Critic*, a journal which owed its inspiration to the Revd William Jones of Nayland – a clergyman wracked by guilt because his ancestor, Colonel Jones, was Oliver Cromwell's brother-in-law and a regicide. In time Jones himself was also to become a contributor to the *Anti-Jacobin Review* [92].

Of course, the loyalist newspapers and journals, like the conservative authors in general, were less concerned with developing ideas about the social contract and the future development of society than they were with challenging the ideas put forward by radicals and restating neo-Burkean ideas of the constitution, of the importance of social morality and of revealed religion, of duty and subservience to church and king, and of respect for the existing social hierarchy and gender relations [39]. When individuals, even the most loyal, embarked on analysing and exploring the authority of the state, the results could be embarrassing. The most striking example of this was John Reeves's *Thoughts on the English Government*, which was published in the form of four 'letters' between 1795 and 1800. Reeves was an attorney with a long career of government service which had included acting as a commissioner of bankrupts, law clerk to the Board of Trade, drafting the aborted Police Bill of 1785, and, most famously, launching the loyalist Association for Preserving Liberty and Property against Republicans and Levellers in November 1792 (see below pp. 31 and 42–4). *Thoughts on the English Government* displayed an unashamed reverence for the monarchy and stressed its importance within the constitutional structure; the two houses of parliament, in Reeves's estimation, were little more than glorious appendages [*Doc. 21*]. Parliament's response to the first letter, spurred by the opposition but also, probably for political expediency, backed by the government, was to charge Reeves with libel. He was acquitted, but did not change his views as the three subsequent letters containing his *Thoughts* were to show – two were published in 1799 and the last in 1800. He never forgave Pitt for the prosecution and for not giving him any public recognition for founding the Association movement; but his access to government patronage and places never suffered – in 1797 he acquired the lucrative position of King's Printer, and between 1803 and 1804 he served as Superintendent of Aliens [85; 92].

Hannah More's thinking was far less contentious and, in the long term, probably far more influential. More had begun her literary career in the 1760s; mixing with the likes of David Garrick and Dr Johnson, she had produced plays and verses which, while relatively successful at the time, are little remembered. By the 1780s her work was taking a much more serious turn; she moved increasingly in evangelical Christian circles and addressed the importance of manners, morals and religion. In 1792 she published *Village Politics*, a well-regarded response to Paine, which was purportedly written by Will Chip, a country carpenter [*Doc. 6a*]. Within three years she had embarked on the project for which she is best remembered, the Cheap Repository Tracts. These tracts were inspired in part by concerns about Painite political material directed at the poorer classes, but the stories and verses were much more than a collection of homilies urging loyalty. The Cheap Repository Tracts were, Susan Pederson has convincingly argued, 'a broad evangelical assault on late eighteenth-century popular culture' [93 *p. 87*]. In contrast to the essentially escapist popular culture found in the chap books which had been sold by pedlars for a century and more, the tracts, while disguised in a popular format, stressed that idleness, intemperance, gambling, and unbelief led to perdition. They emphasised the need for order and hierarchy within families and society; they stressed the importance of marriage and family; and they urged the observance of the strict laws of God by all social classes. The continuation of the Repository by the publisher, when More relinquished her involvement in 1798, suggests that the tracts were, and continued to be, a profitable concern. At least some of the profit came from genteel interest; many respectable individuals appear to have been ready to purchase the tracts and circulate them free to the poor in the hopes of becoming the moral arbiters of popular culture. How many of the less well-to-do accepted, or were won over by, the moral messages, and how many saw them purely in terms of entertainment on the same lines as the chap books, must remain an open question [93; 94; *Doc. 6b*].

In addition to the political and philosophical pamphlets generated by the French Revolution, and More's tracts prompted by rather broader concerns, debate during the 1790s was also joined in sermons, in addresses made in the courts, and in novels. Price's 'On the Love of our Country' was a sermon; the political sermon had a long pedigree, and throughout the 1790s loyalist Anglican clergy preached warnings about the dangers of France, and the need for atonement, especially on the days of fast decreed, periodically, during the war. Some Dissenters, in turn, preached a more radical, reformist gospel [40; 41]. Again it was common for judges and senior magistrates to reflect on political affairs and celebrate the excellence of the British constitution and legal structure in their charges to grand juries at the opening of assizes or quarter sessions. During the 1790s, as before, the more striking of such charges were often printed and circulated for a wider audience [6; *Doc. 14*]. There were significant Jacobin novels, notably Thomas Holcroft's *Anne St. Ives* (1792), William Godwin's *Caleb Williams* (1794) and Robert Bage's *Hermsprong* (1796), each of which provided overt political and social criticism in the mouths and experiences of the central characters. These, in turn, were countered by more than forty anti-Jacobin novels, several of which were written by women determined to participate in the debate. A handful of the anti-Jacobin novels appeared in the early 1790s, and rather more in the period 1798–1805. They tended to understand and portray Jacobinism according to the perceived scale and size of the threat at any given time. Three main strands have been highlighted in their arguments: they appealed directly to the fears of people of property; they portrayed the Jacobin ideology as chimerical and evil; and they stressed the horrors and violence of the revolutionaries, which, in 1798, could also include the experience of the rising in Ireland [149; 151; 153].

Traditional Whig historiography implied that the radicals won the intellectual arguments of the 1790s, but that they were repressed by a British 'terror'. In the last twenty years or so, however, a new consensus has emerged, largely following the lead of H.T. Dickinson. This suggests that a strong faith in the virtues of the British constitution, together with a general resistance to change, meant that radical ideas were defeated as much, if not more so, by the appeal of an innate conservatism rather than by government-sponsored repression [21; 35; 44; 86]. There are difficulties with this new consensus, not the least being the extent to which it can be demonstrated that the arguments of one group were stronger than those of their opponents and the extent to which, during the period of the French Revolution, a new political consciousness was emerging among social groups hitherto excluded from the political nation [36]. Yet, as will become apparent from what follows, there can be little dispute about who were the political victors at least in the short term.

CHAPTER THREE

POLITICS

WHIGS AND OTHERS

The French Revolution led to a significant realignment in British politics. The vestiges of the old Whig Party, which had dominated parliament under the first two Georges, split finally and irrevocably. One group, which gathered around the charismatic figure of Charles James Fox, became isolated and, for a brief period, opted to secede from parliament altogether; the other moved into a coalition with William Pitt the Younger, lost its separate identity and contributed to the emergence of a new political grouping that, subsequently, was to consider itself 'Tory'.

Fox and Pitt were the key figures in British politics for a quarter of a century. Their rivalry was important for the way in which high politics developed over the period, and for the way in which such politics have often been interpreted. Fox saw himself, and was seen by others, as the spokesman for the 'freeborn Englishman' and the guardian of his liberties. He had fostered this reputation during the American War, and particularly when he became member of parliament for the prestigious and populous borough of Westminster. He perpetuated it by showing strong sympathies with the liberal aspirations that were apparent at least in the early stages of the French Revolution. Fox exuded warmth and attracted firm friends and devoted followers, but he was loathed by George III who detested his politics and his ambition. The detestation was mutual. Pitt was a much colder personality. He was equally able, but more pragmatic. He was a master of detail, especially in financial matters. Probably most importantly, for most of his political career he enjoyed the support of George III, something which ensured his grip on office.

George had chosen Pitt as his prime minister in December 1783, ousting a ministry nominally headed by the Duke of Portland, but within which the dominant figures were the veteran Lord North and the young Fox. Pitt was only 23 years old, and he faced a formidable challenge. The country had been defeated in a war seeking to maintain possession of its thirteen American colonies. Old European enemies had joined the colonists. Military failure had prompted a massive extra-parliamentary movement during the war calling for reform. The movement, initially organised by the Revd Christopher Wyvill, had begun in Yorkshire in 1779 among county electors who blamed the war, and particularly the lack of success, on corrupt ministers. The problems, they believed, could be solved by an increase in the number of MPs chosen by the counties; they considered that such men were more independent than those who were elected for the boroughs, and who were elected often as a result of government patronage. While the Association Movement campaigned outside parliament, the opposition within parliament sought to harness the agitation for what was called 'economical reform' – a reduction in government patronage and sinecures in order to restore the independence of the House of Commons. In the event, remarkably little was achieved immediately and while demands for reform continued to be heard, the extra-parliamentary agitation had largely subsided when Pitt became prime minister.

Pitt himself had espoused reform and, as prime minister, he introduced a modest plan for parliamentary reform along the lines sought by Wyvill and the petitioning campaign. However, when in April 1785 the Commons rejected the plan, by 248 votes to 174, he shelved the idea; and losing a bill in parliament was not a resigning matter for a relatively popular principal minister who still had the king's confidence and support. For the remainder of the 1780s parliamentary reform was dormant and Pitt focused his attentions on financial retrenchment and repairing the damage wrought by the disastrous war for America. His financial reforms were concerned with preserving and improving the existing system; it was never his intention significantly to change or to dismantle the Hanoverian 'military-fiscal state' which, over the preceding hundred years with the exception of the American war, had revealed itself to be an effective machine and generally superior to its European rivals. Pitt himself had a reputation for probity and opposition to faction, and as the 1780s wore on he acquired a reputation for being the responsible manager of the state apparatus and its tax money. But Pitt's reforms did nothing to limit the opportunities for the ruling elite and its agents to feather their nests at the public expense. As Philip Harling has forcefully argued, he 'had neither the will nor the inclination to keep able but ambitious officials from reaching for as many emoluments as they could lay their hands on' [47 *p. 63*]. This was largely masked until a new war broke out.

Following the general election of 1790 Pitt's government could count on an overall majority of about 160 in the Commons. But the government was not established on a party basis; indeed, Pitt was not the leader of a political party. He depended on the support of the king; this provided him with opportunities for constructing a government, for bolstering his personal support in the Commons and it gave him the support of the unattached MPs who generally could be relied upon to support the king's choice of first minister. Pitt was also adept at cultivating conscientious back-benchers, opinion-formers and experts on particular issues. He used such men to dominate parliamentary committees and to maintain a tight control over parliamentary business. He also scrupulously planned the tactics to be deployed in key debates [45; 46]. Parties, in the sense of organised bodies with secretariats and paid-up members did not exist in eighteenth-century Britain. An assessment of the structure of the House of Commons made in 1788 concluded that Pitt had 52 MPs attached to his 'Party', and that were he no longer prime minister, not more than 20 of these would be returned. Fox, in contrast, was credited with a 'Party' of 138. Another 185 members were described as the 'Party of the Crown' who could be expected to support the government under any principal minister who had the confidence of the king and who was not peculiarly unpopular.

Yet if parties in the modern sense did not exist, those members of parliament who assembled behind Fox, together with another score or so and an influential group of grandees in the House of Lords, saw themselves as united by ideology into what they considered to be the Whig Party. Pitt always considered himself to be an 'independent Whig', but for the first ten years of his premiership the Whig Party constituted the main body of the opposition to his ministry. These Whigs resented the way in which George III had chosen Pitt as first minister and had engineered their downfall in 1783–84. On the eve of the Revolution in France, Portland was still recognised as head of this 'party'; Fox was its main spokesman in the Commons.

The potential for a split among the Whigs over events in France first became publicly apparent early in 1790. Fox generally spoke sympathetically about the Revolution, while Edmund Burke was highly critical. Burke was already dissatisfied with, and becoming marginalised by, the party. He considered that his colleagues were lax over the impeachment proceedings against Warren Hastings for aggression and extortion while Governor General in India. More seriously, he had been appalled by the opportunism of Fox and his friends during George III's illness in 1788–89 when they had argued against Pitt's Regency Bill on the grounds that it would unfairly limit the hereditary royal power of the Prince of Wales as Regent. In Burke's eyes, such opposition was contrary to traditional Whig constitutional beliefs regarding both the monarchy and parliament. The first serious clash on the French Revolution came during the debate on the Army Estimates in February 1790. Fox opposed any increase, expressing his belief in the peaceful attitudes of foreign powers. Burke took the opposite view. The new principles to be found in France, he insisted, constituted a potential and very serious threat. In the following month, when Fox urged the repeal of the Test and Corporation Acts which barred Protestant Dissenters from political life, Burke warned that such a change posed a threat to the Established Church and drew parallels with France where, he alleged, the Church had become the victim of plunder and robbery. The final break came in May the following year; and when it came it was public and painful. During a debate on the government of Quebec, in which the French Revolution again figured in their arguments, Burke declared his friendship with Fox to be 'at an end'. Fox himself was so overcome with emotion that he could not respond.

While Burke was the first to break publicly with Fox, other Whigs were unhappy about his sympathy for the French Revolution. Their concerns grew when, in the summer of 1791, the Revolution appeared to take a radical lurch following Louis XVI's unsuccessful flight from the country and his apprehension at Varennes. These concerns increased still further when in April 1792 a group of young, radical members of the party established the Association of the Friends of the People. Fox himself was not a member of the Association, but he neither discouraged nor repudiated it. On 30 April Charles Grey, a spokesman for the Association and the future Lord Grey whose government would pass the Great Reform Act, informed the Commons of his intention of bringing a motion for parliamentary reform before the next session. Grey gave no inkling of specific proposals. It seems probable that the Association had, as yet, no precise plans. This gave opponents the opportunity to suggest that the intentions might be unconstitutional and subversive, and that the Association was intending to stir up discontent within the country.

Pitt's government could not but be aware of the Whigs' problems. At some point, probably in early May 1792, overtures were made towards one of the Whig grandees, Lord Loughborough, about the possibility of leaders of the opposition meeting with the government to consider important political matters. Possibly the government was concerned about the emergence of popular radicalism; probably also ministers thought the opportunity too good to miss of dividing the opposition and bringing some over to their side. Pitt was experiencing difficulties with his Lord Chancellor, Lord Thurlow; Loughborough was a potential candidate for the post, and it was known that he very much wanted it. The result of the approaches was Portland's very general agreement to act in 'concert' with the government over matters such as the Royal Proclamation on Seditious Writings, issued on 21 May, but he was not prepared to work in 'conjunction' with Pitt. Manoeuvring continued throughout the early summer and there was talk of a coalition, but it was also clear that it was unlikely that any government could be formed in which Pitt and Fox would be prepared to work together. Pitt offered honours and non-governmental posts to Portland and the conservative Whigs. Portland and Fox struggled to hold their party together.

Again it was events in France which accentuated the Whigs' divisions. In the late summer and autumn of 1792 came news of the September Massacres, of French victories and of aggressive decrees from the National Convention. In January 1793 Loughborough accepted the seals as Lord Chancellor. The execution of Louis XVI in that same month and, shortly afterwards, the French declaration of war, left Fox and his supporters even more exposed and isolated. Forty-five members resigned from the Whig Club, severing all ties with Fox and proposing a closer understanding with the government. William Windham, who took an attitude towards the Revolution similar to that of Burke, led a group of about 25 Whigs into a 'Third Party', agreeing to support the government over the war but reserving judgement over other matters. Grey's motion for reform, introduced into the Commons on 6 May 1793, did not put forward precise proposals and specifically rejected the principle of universal suffrage, but its defeat by 283 votes to 41 demonstrated how isolated the group which clustered around Fox was becoming and how hostile the majority in parliament was to such proposals.

Of course, it was in the interests of Pitt and his ministers to play upon the split within the Whig Party, but the way in which they cultivated the conservative Whigs during 1793 and 1794 is also indicative of the increasing concerns with which they regarded events in France and the emergence of popular radicalism in Britain. Pitt and key ministers like Henry Dundas did not share Burke's single-minded hostility to French principles. Yet they appear to have become increasingly worried by the direction of events in France during 1792, especially when, towards the end of the year, decrees from the National Convention threatened to sponsor internal disorder. The precise reasoning behind the Royal Proclamation of May 1792 against seditious writings is difficult to explain. But there had been trouble when radicals sought to celebrate Bastille Day in the previous year (see below pp. 40–1), Painite radicalism appeared to be agitating the minds of many outside established political society, events in France were providing an unsettling example of radical plebeian activism, and nervous conservatives began to see revolution lurking in every project from religious toleration to the abolition of the slave trade [*Doc.* 7]. A second Royal Proclamation, issued on 1 December, deplored the ineffectiveness of its predecessor and mobilised the militia. This Proclamation was issued against a background of industrial disorder in the provinces, rumours of political trouble on the streets of London, the threat of a general increase in the cost of foodstuffs, and a worsening diplomatic situation with a militarily successful and aggressively proselytising Republican France [48; 65].

The Portland Whigs were as concerned as members of Pitt's ministry about the success of Jacobinism in France and its apparent emergence in Britain. At the beginning of 1794 Portland and his followers decided to adopt a line in parliament similar to that of the 'Third Party'; in July a formal coalition was agreed, and the terms were such that Pitt's government now took on the aura of a government of national unity. Four leading Whigs entered the Cabinet – Portland himself as home secretary, Earl Fitzwilliam as Lord President of the Council, Earl Spencer as Lord Privy Seal, and William Windham as secretary at war. Some of Pitt's supporters considered that he had been too generous in the distribution of offices. Portland's friends thoroughly approved of the arrangement, though their separate identity as Whigs rapidly disappeared. Fox was greatly distressed and felt betrayed by old friends and colleagues [54; 59].

Both Portland and Windham were inclined to take a hard line against Jacobinism at home and abroad and these two particularly provided a stiffening for the government's behaviour in this respect. They encouraged closer links with French *émigré* groups and urged support for the restoration of the Bourbon monarchy in France as a specific war aim. In the Commons, Fox's support shrank to a rump of no more than 60 MPs, and sometimes to as few as 35. These could mainly unite around opposition to the war, concern about the influence of the Crown, support for civil and religious liberties, and an intense dislike of Pitt; many of them also shared a broad desire for reform. Fox's distress led him into bouts of lethargy. He consoled himself by drawing parallels with the American war when military disaster had brought the collapse of the government and his own brief opportunity for ministerial office; but history was not to repeat itself. During 1795 he was active in promoting petitions against the war and then against the Two Acts which put restrictions on both public meetings and free speech. He was similarly active during the general election of 1796 when, in spite of a lack of co-ordination and less money to spend than in previous contests, the Foxites forged significant if, ultimately, transient links with opponents of the war across the country. Failure in the challenge to the Two Acts and in the attempt to shift the majority in parliament led to increasing bouts of depression and inaction on Fox's part, and he began contemplating secession from parliament.

In the spring of 1797, when the war appeared to be going particularly badly with French invasion fleets off Ireland, a small landing in Wales, and a run on the banks, Fox was again active in promoting a petitioning campaign outside parliament. He hoped to build on a move within parliament by a group of MPs who were not Foxite but who were increasingly of the belief that negotiations with France were essential though impossible as long as Pitt, Grenville and others remained in the government. This group was not contemplating replacing Pitt with Fox; indeed it is not clear who they saw as taking over as chief minister. But for Fox and his supporters this provided an opportunity to take their case to the country, and to win the backing of disillusioned electors who would join in petitioning the king for the removal of his ministers. The campaign had some initial success in London, but when it moved into the counties it began to stall. There simply was not the support for which they, and some old county reformers like Christopher Wyvill, had hoped. While attempts to rouse the provinces continued, encouraged by Fox, Grey brought forward a new motion for parliamentary reform. On this occasion, May 1797, Grey presented a specific plan which had echoes of that introduced by Pitt a dozen years before. He disavowed manhood suffrage, but proposed triennial parliaments, a slight extension of the franchise in the counties, a uniform franchise in the boroughs, and a reorganisation of seats. The motion was rejected by 256 votes to 91, and while reform had secured a better showing than four years earlier, Fox concluded that secession from parliament was the only viable means of protesting against the government and the majority.

Pitt rode out the tide of opposition and announced proposals for Anglo-Austrian talks from which, it was implied, negotiations with the French might begin. In June, preliminary discussions were begun with the French. The Foxite secession did not mean, however, that the government escaped criticism and opposition. Moreover, two determined, eloquent Foxites continued to take their seats. William Smith and George Tierney considered secession an abrogation of responsibility. Smith was a Dissenter from a merchant family who had moved from being a supporter of Pitt to the Foxite camp in 1792. Tierney was a young, ambitious politician; he had principles, but he also had an eye to maintaining his precarious hold on his volatile Southwark constituency. A third notable Foxite, the playwright Richard Brinsley Sheridan, also attended from time to time.

Increases in taxes to fight the war were never popular, and it seems probable that early in 1798, in order to deflect dissatisfaction with increases announced in the assessed taxes, the government set out to blacken its political opponents by drawing attention to their dangerous principles – and the opposition played into Pitt's hands by providing the opportunities for this. In January, at a dinner to celebrate Fox's birthday, the Duke of Norfolk toasted 'The health of our sovereign – the majesty of the people'. He was promptly dismissed as Lord Lieutenant of the West Riding and commander of that county's militia regiment. When, a few weeks later, Fox offered a similar toast, he was deprived of his seat on the Privy Council. In May, Pitt clashed with Tierney in the Commons over the Navy Bill. Pitt accused Tierney of seeking to impede the defence of the nation. Tierney responded with a challenge and the two duelled with pistols on Putney Heath. Neither was injured, but honour was satisfied.

The intense dislike between Pitt and the Foxites was personal, but it was also entangled in attitudes to the constitution and the French Revolution. George III considered that Fox's attitude and behaviour made him an 'enemy' of the country. In the aftermath of his toast to the sovereignty of the people in January 1798, Pitt contemplated having Fox committed to the Tower of London for his behaviour. Such extreme action is hardly likely to have been considered purely out of personal pique or simply as a way to besmirch the Foxite opposition. At the close of 1792 Fox had boasted that he could and would divide the House of Commons on any proposal brought forward by Pitt. This was opposition for the sake of opposition, and while it would be difficult to prove that it had any precise impact on the eventual emergence of a two-party system in Britain, it can certainly be seen as a precedent. It was, however, not the Foxite opposition that eventually brought Pitt's downfall, but the loss of the king's support.

In the aftermath of the 1798 rebellion (see below pp. 51–2) Pitt saw, even more urgently, the need to pacify the Irish. The best solution, he believed, was the union of Britain and Ireland, and the corollary of that was Catholic emancipation. The former appeared far easier to achieve than the latter, and the union was successfully established in 1800. Pitt then began serious discussions about emancipation with his ministers; some were uncertain, others were opposed, but the biggest stumbling block was George III. Officially the king was not told about the plans, but Lord Loughborough, an opponent of the idea, informed him. At the royal levée on 28 January 1801 a furious monarch let Henry Dundas know that he would have none of it.

Pitt had weathered serious opposition before, and even defeats in parliament. On this occasion, however, he chose resignation. Why? Three principal reasons have been suggested. First, his health was bad. The pressures of running the country for nearly 20 years, and most recently during a war of an unprecedented scale, had left him mentally and physically exhausted; nor were matters helped by his heavy drinking. Secondly, for all his faults, Pitt was a patriot. It is possible that he chose to resign in the belief that peace was necessary for the country, but that it would be impossible for successful negotiations to be concluded with the French as long as he remained prime minister. There is some evidence that he had considered resignation during the dark days of 1797. In 1801 the internal situation was, arguably, even worse with the country wracked by food shortages and domestic unrest (see below pp. 38–9 and 67–8). Thirdly, following George III's response to the plan for Catholic emancipation it was probably clear to Pitt that others now had the king's ear and that if he stayed on as prime minister he would only have nominal power. This last may have been the most significant reason for Pitt's departure from office though, as ever in the assessment of personal decisions, it is probably most sensible to consider his action as the result of a combination of elements [46, vol. III *pp. 515–16*].

George III chose Henry Addington, Speaker of the Commons, to replace Pitt. By October 1801 Addington had successfully negotiated the preliminaries of the Peace of Amiens with the French. The peace proved to be only a temporary respite. Hostilities were resumed in May 1803; Addington resigned a year later, and George recalled Pitt. Within two years, however, Pitt was dead, worn out by the pressures of office; and though Pitt's death gave Fox the opportunity to serve in government as foreign secretary in the 'Ministry of All the Talents', before the close of 1806 he too was dead. The 'Talents', as the name implies, was a broad-based government; its short life of 14 months provided the Foxite tradition of Whigs with their only experience of government between 1783 and 1827. The downfall of the Talents, brought about once again by George III's opposition to Catholic emancipation, heralded a succession of governments composed of Pittites who gradually began to assume the name of Tory. They continued the war against France with Pittite policies of organising and financing coalitions, with seaborne adventures across the wider world, but also supporting a British army on continental Europe fighting with increasing confidence and success under the Duke of Wellington. They also continued to take a firm line against popular radicalism.

RADICALS AND REPRESSION

There was a long and lively tradition of popular political culture in eighteenth-century England. Crowds, and not necessarily just crowds of electors, gathered to see candidates nominated for elections, to hear them on the hustings, and to celebrate their victories. Heroes were chaired in triumph; opponents were jeered and burned in effigy. The American war and the John Wilkes affair in particular appear to have extended the numbers within the nation who were politically aware far beyond those who had the vote. In addition, there was a long tradition of clubs which involved the unenfranchised. Convivial clubs, debating clubs, trade clubs all met regularly in taverns. The excitement generated by the French Revolution built on these traditions and developments. Most significantly in this respect, it fostered the growth of radical political clubs and societies. In these societies skilled artisans and working men rubbed shoulders with a few radical lawyers and other professional men; they debated constitutional and contemporary political issues, and they called for political reform. The first of these popular radical societies was probably the Sheffield Society for Constitutional Information, established towards the end of 1791. It drew the bulk of its membership from journeymen and masters in the cutlery trades [*Doc. 9*]. It also benefited from the support of men like Joseph Gales, the editor of the *Sheffield Register*. The *Register* provided the society with an organ for the dissemination of ideas, and the paper's printing press could also be used for the society's own handbills and notices. But if the Sheffield Society was the first such group, the most celebrated was the London Corresponding Society (LCS) established in a public house in the Strand in January 1792.

The key figure in the creation of the LCS was Thomas Hardy, a 40-year-old Scottish shoemaker who had been living and working in London for some ten years. Hardy became the society's first secretary and treasurer. His interest in reform had been fostered by reading some old political pamphlets published at the time of the American war by the Society for Constitutional Information (SCI), a club of reformist gentlemen which had been established in 1780 at the peak of the reform campaign. Hardy initially intended that membership of the LCS should be confined to the un-enfranchised, but he soon came round to the opinion that this would make it too limited. The weekly subscription of one penny meant that artisans and journeymen could easily become members and participate in the debates and discussions; but the meetings were also open to men of greater means, like Maurice Margarot, a merchant who had been educated at the University of Geneva and who was appointed the society's chairman in May. The society also drew on support, encouragement and advice from the revived SCI, and in particular from gentlemen reformers like the Revd John Horne Tooke. At the beginning of April 1792, with a membership of about 70 meeting in small divisions usually in London pubs, the LCS presented an address to the public with a set of resolutions outlining its aims [*Doc. 8*].

The LCS took its name from its intention to correspond with other, like-minded groups across the kingdom. It opened a correspondence with the SCI in March, and was soon in touch with other societies in Norwich, Sheffield and elsewhere. In their desire for 'constitutional information', the corresponding societies read and debated the political pamphlets of the day. They built upon the traditional ideas of the freeborn Englishman, but also upon religious Dissent; Norwich in particular was a hot-bed of Dissent and this fed significantly into the city's radicalism. But above all, the artisans and journeymen of the new popular clubs were inspired by Paine's *Rights of Man*. Cheap, sometimes abridged copies were published for, and devoured by, members. But the popularity of Paine among these plebeian reformers alarmed some of the gentlemen who had campaigned for reform ten years earlier. Some members of the SCI resigned their membership. Wyvill himself deplored Paine's 'unconstitutional ground' and lamented that he had 'formed a party for a Republic among the lower classes of people by holding out to them the prospect of plundering the rich' [quoted in 23 *p. 28*]. Pitt's government appears also to have been concerned and responded to the interest in Paine with the Royal Proclamation of 21 May 1792 which warned people to be on their guard against seditious writings and urged magistrates to discover the authors and printers.

The Proclamation brought forth nearly 400 loyal petitions but seems to have had little impact on the new radicalism. The popular societies continued their activities throughout the summer of 1792 and into the autumn. Their numbers appear to have grown steadily. They sought to defend and explain the violence of the Revolution in France [*Doc. 10b*], they rejoiced at the victories of the French armies, they raised subscriptions for the 'soldiers of liberty' and the LCS, in conjunction with other societies, transmitted a congratulatory address to the National Convention early in November [*Doc. 11*]. These activities, together with worsening relations between the British government and the government in Paris, combined to prompt a loyalist reaction.

The Royal Proclamation of 1 December once more urged magistrates to act against seditious publications. The government considered introducing new legislation to clarify the law regarding sedition, but opted instead for encouraging local action under the existing law. Such local action was encouraged, in turn, by the successful prosecution of Paine *in absentia*; legally, this prosecution clarified the seditious nature of his works. Further action against radicalism and 'sedition' came through the development of loyalist associations. The Associations for the Preservation of Liberty and Property Against Republicans and Levellers originated in a plan prepared by John Reeves who, in November 1792, had only recently returned from a brief spell acting as the chief justice of a court in Newfoundland. Pitt and his ministers were unaware of Reeves's proposals before their publication on 23 November, but seized upon them as adaptable to, and useful for, their own ends [88]. Loyalist associations sprang up across the country; some were patriotic groups which embraced all facets of opinion – Fox himself belonged to the committee of the Association of St George's, Hanover Square, together with William Windham [85; 90; 91]. But others were determined to foster an aggressive, anti-Painite loyalism. They organised demonstrations in which Paine was burned in effigy; they published and otherwise circulated loyalist literature; in some instances they organised prosecutions for sedition, sometimes also organising the jury to ensure a conviction (see below p. 43).

The Reeves societies, a spate of prosecutions of printers for publishing seditious libels, threats of such prosecutions which publishers and booksellers sometimes avoided by public apologies [*Doc. 16*], threats to publicans who opened their doors to the popular clubs that they might lose their licence if such meetings were allowed to continue, and the outbreak of war, all served as a check upon popular radicalism in 1793, but by no means did they extinguish it. Thirty six petitions were presented to parliament to coincide with Grey's motion for reform in May; 24 of these came from Scotland and it was to Scotland, towards the end of 1793, that the focus of radical activity was switched.

The system of parliamentary representation in Scotland was extremely narrow. Whereas perhaps as many as one man in ten in England and Wales had the vote, in Scotland it was less than one in a hundred. Furthermore, political patronage was firmly entrenched and expertly employed by Henry Dundas [113; 114]. Scottish reformers had been active during the American war, and the reform movement had gained renewed vigour in the early 1790s. At the end of 1793 a convention of reformers was summoned in Edinburgh, and societies in England were invited to send delegates. The English delegates arrived late, but reorganised the meeting into a British Convention which adopted many French practices – notably referring to each other as 'citizen'. Convention was a word with a long English pedigree but, given that it was the French National Convention which had ordered the execution of Louis XVI and declared war on Britain, it was not the most fortunate of titles. The Edinburgh authorities rapidly closed the meetings. They had already prosecuted two leading reformers, Thomas Muir, a young lawyer, and the Revd Thomas Fyshe Palmer, a dissenting minister, before an openly hostile judge and a packed jury. The leaders of the Convention followed: William Skirving its secretary, and Maurice Margarot and Joseph Gerrald, the two delegates from the LCS. Like Muir and Palmer, they too were found guilty and sentenced to be transported to Botany Bay.

The prosecutions of the 'Scottish Martyrs' stung the English radical societies into renewed activity. There was agitated correspondence between the LCS and other societies [*Doc. 17*]. Mass meetings were held in London and Sheffield. Plans were made for a new British Convention to be held in the summer of 1794. The spies who had infiltrated the LCS on the government's behalf began to report talk of arming and drilling. On 12 May the government acted. Thomas Hardy and Daniel Adams, the secretary of the SCI, were arrested; other arrests followed. A parliamentary committee of secrecy was established to investigate the popular societies. Legislation was rushed through parliament to suspend the Habeas Corpus Act with reference to any individuals accused of treason and arrested on a warrant signed by one of the secretaries of state or by six members of the privy council.

About two dozen individuals were held under the suspension of the Habeas Corpus Act in England but, as the government and its law officers interrogated their prisoners and their spies, and prepared the cases for prosecution, two Scots were arrested, charged and tried for high treason. The evidence deployed against David Downie and Robert Watt in Edinburgh suggested a pretty feeble conspiracy at best; and it was revealed that Watt had acted as a government informer until August 1793. Yet both were found guilty and sentenced to be hanged, drawn and quartered. Downie was reprieved; Watt was executed in October 1794, though he was spared the full excess of the punishment.

Only three of those arrested in England were tried: Hardy, Horne Tooke, and the young radical lecturer John Thelwall. All were acquitted; and their successive acquittals at the Old Bailey in November and December 1794 were greeted with jubilation by London crowds; and while Windham branded them 'acquitted felons', all the other prisoners were released. Several reasons can be advanced for the failure of the government's case. First, there was no direct evidence that those brought to trial were actually threatening the life of the king or the existence of the constitution. The attorney general's case was one of 'constructive treason'; in other words, he argued not that the accused actually intended the overthrow of the existing system, but rather that, had their plans been brought to fruition then the result would have been such. Arguments such as these were complex; the opening speech for the prosecution took nine hours, and probably lost the jurymen's understanding in the process. In Thomas Erskine, the Foxite MP for Portsmouth, the accused had one of the finest advocates of the day, and Erskine excelled himself in his conduct of the defence. Finally, the jury was probably reluctant to find for the Crown since the charge of treason still brought the capital sentence of hanging, drawing and quartering. Eighteenth-century jurors commonly brought verdicts to fit their personal assessment of the accused and of the charges brought against them. Even if the pathetic Watt had only been hanged and subsequently beheaded, the prospect of seeing men executed for the *possible* outcome of their actions was likely to have been much more than many respectable men of property, serving as jurors, were prepared to have on their consciences [83].

There was a belief among many radicals that convictions in the treason trials would have unleashed a ferocious repression. The acquittals, in consequence, were received with relief and with rejoicing that one of the central rights of the freeborn Englishman, the right of a trial by jury, had not yet been subverted [*Doc. 18*]. The LCS did not keep minutes of its meetings for the first half of 1795, possibly fearing a renewed offensive by the government. And the government remained nervous. In March it arrested, and eventually had committed to an asylum, Richard Brothers, a millenarial prophet who claimed descent from King David and, directly, from James, one of the brothers of Jesus. Brothers's prophesies of the world's doom fed on anxieties about the war and the poor harvest and seriously agitated crowds in London. James Gillray, the great political caricaturist, caught the mood of the moment with 'Presages of the Millennium', in which the pale rider of the Apocalypse – in this case a naked Pitt riding the white horse of Hanover – tramples Foxites and a herd of pigs – the latter being an allusion to Burke's reference in his *Reflections* to 'the swinish multitude' [*Doc. 29b*].

By the summer of 1795, the LCS was making its presence felt once again with public activity and petitions, and building on public anxieties. Throughout the summer and autumn it thrived. To its call for parliamentary reform were now added demands for peace with France and for action to deal with the serious food shortages. The failure to make peace and the food shortages were both blamed on the corrupt parliamentary and governmental system. On 26 October, a mass, open-air meeting was held in a field near Copenhagen House, Islington. Thousands attended – estimates ranged from 40,000 to 100,000 – to hear speeches from Thelwall and LCS leaders such as John Gale Jones, a surgeon and man-midwife, and John Binns, an Irish-born plumber. An address was presented to the nation, a remonstrance to the king, and a series of resolutions was passed [*Doc. 23*]. Three days later, as he rode in state to open parliament, George III was jeered by a crowd calling for bread and peace, and the window of his coach was broken. On his return journey he was attacked again. Pitt's government responded with two new pieces of legislation: the first bill made actions against the king's person or his heirs capital offences, and extended the law of treason to include inciting hatred of the king, his heirs, his government or the constitution, though the punishment here was restricted to transportation; the second bill restricted public meetings to 50 persons, unless a magistrate had given permission in advance, and it also gave magistrates wide powers over lecture rooms and radical lecturers.

The attack on the king and the two bills excited a new wave of political activity across the country. Congratulatory addresses were sent to George on his escape, but many of these also called for an end to the war and protested against the two bills as being inimicable to the Englishman's boasted rights and liberties. In addition to the congratulatory addresses, there were petitions calling specifically for peace and for a withdrawal of the bills. It was not just Foxite Whigs and popular radicals who organised the petitions. Indeed, in the provinces the leadership of the petition campaign was taken by men who increasingly styled themselves as the 'Friends of Peace'. These men, according to J.E. Cookson, 'represented a body of liberal opinion which had been shaped and hardened since about 1770 by opposition to clerical subscription to the Thirty-Nine Articles, the American war and the slave trade, and support for moderate parliamentary reform and the repeal of the Test and Corporation Acts' [62 *p. 2*]. They included men like Wyvill, and men from the 'middling sort' throughout the provinces, like Thomas Bigge, a Newcastle lawyer, Ralph Fenwick, a Durham doctor, William Roscoe and his circle in Liverpool. They sought to establish some middle ground between radicalism and loyalism, urging a raft of moderate reforms and an end to corruption.

The petitioning campaign against the two bills was a failure; on 18 December, just over a month after their introduction, they received royal assent. Both the British Jacobins and their historians have stressed the significance of the new legislation in undermining popular radicalism. It was not that the Acts were much used, but rather that members of the popular societies drifted away, some frightened, some disillusioned. The LCS sought to revive and maintain correspondence with clubs elsewhere in the country. It sent delegates to encourage provincial clubs; both Binns and Gale Jones were arrested for such activities in 1796. It established its *Moral and Political Magazine* in July of that year, designed to extend constitutional knowledge and revive the society's finances; unfortunately the venture served only to extend the society's debts. Regardless of the new legislation on public meetings, John Thelwall attempted to continue his radical lectures, but found loyalist mobs ready to break up such gatherings, apparently with the tacit approval of local magistrates. Indeed it appears that naval officers were behind an anti-Thelwall mob in Great Yarmouth hoping to press-gang him and, according to one rumour, to put him on a Russian ship bound for Siberia [81; *Doc. 24*].

However, while popular radicalism subsided during 1796 and early 1797, dissatisfaction was growing among the thousands of seamen cooped up below decks on the battle fleets. Early in 1797, a petition circulated among the men on the warships anchored at Spithead, complaining particularly about pay and conditions. Several copies were then sent from different ships to admirals and the admiralty. The petitions were ignored and the admiralty considered that the best way to scotch the trouble was to order the fleet to sea. But when the order was given on 16 April the crews mutinied and the ships remained in port. The government responded rapidly with concessions to the men; though not rapidly and clearly enough for the angry crews who renewed the mutiny for a week in May. As the crews in Spithead called off their action, those in the Thames anchorage of the Nore, fearful that they were excluded from the agreement, began their own action. The Nore mutiny was a much more bitter affair, involving a blockade of the Thames. And when the mutiny ended in mid-June, the government responded with ferocity; 36 men were executed, and ten times that number flogged or sent to serve for the rest of their lives in the colonies [68; 71; 82]

There were concerns that the mutinies had been fomented by popular radicals. The government sent agents to the ports to investigate; no conclusive evidence could be found, though some links seem likely. At Spithead the original petitions were relatively simply phrased with straightforward requests. Some of the language used at the Nore, however, appears rather more high-flown and contains clear echoes of radical ideology and phraseology [*Doc. 25*]. Moreover as the Nore mutiny drew to its desperate conclusion there was talk among some ship's delegates of sailing the fleet over to the enemy. It does not, of course, require an entire workforce to be committed to a radical ideology for industrial action to take on a political hue; and it is erroneous to assume that industrial action in time of national crisis is simply the result of the gullible being led astray by agitators and demagogues. The boredom of life on board ship, aggravated by frustration over a long, unsuccessful war, by poor pay and conditions, and by concerns for families at home who had only recently had to cope with serious food shortages, were sufficient in themselves to provoke anger and discontent, and to encourage political and economic discussion among messmates. The fleet mutinies of 1797 might well be seen as a mild prefiguration of events 120 years later at Kronstadt and Kiel.

In 1798 there was an attempt to repeat the mutinies. This time the agitation was overtly political and was largely, though not entirely, the work of United Irishmen. While Irishmen were over-represented in the fleet, they were insufficient to ensure the success of these mutinies. Moreover, the aggressive anti-Protestantism of at least some of the mutineers [*Doc. 26*] was in itself sufficient to divide them from Protestant Irish and from most English and Scots seamen [82 *pp.145–51*].

By 1798 some of the popular radicals in England appear to have been linking with the United Irishmen and dabbling with plans for some sort of insurrectionary activity. It is always difficult for historians to penetrate the secret world of political conspiracy. Radicals who live to an old age and write their memoirs might seek to modify the rash behaviour of their youth, and to emphasise their own respectability in contrast to unsavoury government spies and an unscrupulous government. Spies can write reports containing what they think the government wishes to read rather than what they have actually observed; they might also embroider their reports to keep themselves in business. Governments can seek to blow conspiracies out of all proportion in order to strengthen their own position, to tarnish constitutional opponents, or even to cover their own gullibility in accepting scare stories from their spies. The traditional Whig and Fabian historians of radicalism, trades unions and the progress of parliamentary reform, tended to dismiss the stories of revolutionary activity among the working class as something confined to a tiny, lunatic fringe. But in *The Making of the English Working Class*, E.P. Thompson suggested, probably rightly, that these stories needed to be taken much more seriously; ever since historians have argued about just how seriously [13; 30; 82; 97; 99].

On 28 February 1798, John Binns was arrested in Margate seeking a ship for France. There were four other Irishmen in company with Binns, notably Arthur O'Connor, one of the more fiery leaders of the United Irishmen, and the Revd James Coigley, a Catholic priest. A treasonable address to the French was found in Coigley's pocket. All five were charged with treason. One historian of the United Irishmen has concluded that 'there was sufficient secret evidence to convict all five, but channels of information ... were too valuable to reveal in open court' [107 *p. 184*]. At the trial, held at the Maidstone Assizes in May, Fox, Sheridan and other leading Whigs appeared as character witnesses for O'Connor, while O'Connor himself shifted the burden of guilt on to Coigley. The jury found a guilty verdict only against Coigley. He was executed, while the others walked free, though in Binns's and O'Connor's cases freedom was only temporary. Moreover, O'Connor's subsequent confession, along with that of other United Irish leaders, revealed the extent of his involvement with revolutionary activity.

The arrests in Margate coincided with increasing information being passed to the government about new organisations going by the names of United Englishmen, United Scotsmen and, sometimes, United Britons, all with close links to the United Irishmen. These groups were rumoured to be arming, and from Manchester in particular there were reports of United Englishmen seeking to infiltrate and to recruit from among the soldiers quartered in the district. Through men like Binns there appeared to be close links between the United Irishmen, the United Englishmen and the LCS. Arrests had been made in Scotland in November 1797. Arrests were made in London and Manchester in April 1798, and the Habeas Corpus Act was suspended once again. The period 1797–1800 was labelled by Francis Place, the radical tailor and himself a young, but leading member of the LCS, as the English 'Reign of Terror'.

> A disloyal word was enough to bring down punishment upon any man's head; laughing at the awkwardness of a volunteer corps was criminal, people were apprehended and sent on board a man of war for this breach of decorum, which was punished as a terrible crime.
>
> (British Library, Add. MSS 27808 fol. 110)

There is probably an element of exaggeration here. Self-dramatisation has been described as the 'characteristic vice of the English Jacobins' [80 *p. 134*]. Nevertheless these years were hard and unpleasant for the popular radicals. There were one or two exemplary prosecutions, such as that of Gilbert Wakefield for a seditious libel: Wakefield, a classical scholar, suggested that the government had not negotiated with the French in good faith, that the army was made up of vagabonds and outcasts, that the militia and Volunteers were not keen to fight, and that the poverty and wretchedness of the poor would actually assist the French invasion [66; 75]. A few less well-known individuals were prosecuted for uttering seditious words; probably many more were detained and investigated for a brief period, and then released without trial but no doubt severely shaken by their experience, if not contrite [103]. Following the arrests of radical leaders in Manchester and London in April 1798, and another series of arrests in the next year, about three dozen men were held, under the suspension of the Habeas Corpus Act without trial, for between two and three years.

In addition to the arrests, the trials, and the suspension of the Habeas Corpus Act, parliament passed a series of other measures designed to prevent subversion and to suppress political activity by members of the plebeian classes. In the aftermath of the naval mutinies, which were followed by rumours of attempts to subvert the soldiery, the government passed an Act making any attempt to incite mutiny a capital offence. Another Act, passed shortly afterwards, made the administering and taking of unlawful oaths an offence punishable by seven years' transportation. In the summer of 1799, the Suppression of Seditious and Treasonable Societies Act banned the United Societies and the LCS by name. The latter received the royal assent on the same day as the first Combination Act which made any workmen who organised industrial activity liable to a brief summary trial before a magistrate [67].

It is tempting to see the coincidence of the banning of the popular radical societies and the Combination Act, with its amending legislation of 1800, as a concerted effort against all forms of activity by plebeian groups, economic as well as political. Yet the Combination Act did not make illegal something which had previously been legal. What it did was to bring any attempt by workers, and in 1800 also by masters, to combine in restraint of trade within the remit of the summary jurisdiction of magistrates' courts; the penalties were not great compared with those available at quarter sessions or assize courts, but the justice administered was cheap and speedy. As well as part of an assault against plebeian activity, the Combination Act can also be seen as an indication of the state decreeing its withdrawal from a traditional role in the field of wage regulation; this was partly a reflection of the triumph of Smithian economics, but it was equally an admission that, given the rapidly changing economy, Acts which had previously permitted magistrates to regulate different trades were now becoming both unthinkable and unworkable [74 *esp. pp. 57–60*]. Like the other repressive legislation of Pitt's government, the Combination Acts do not appear to have been greatly used, but they probably had an influence discouraging at least some organisation among workers.

But how, overall, did radicalism respond in general to the repressive assault of 1798–1800? In 1799 and again in 1800 there were poor harvests and once again crowds took to the streets and the markets demanding bread at an affordable price, punishing some farmers, corn-factors, millers and bakers, and threatening others. Again, and perhaps more often and with greater vehemence, threatening letters and notices employed the language and imagery of the French Revolution [*Doc. 27a–d*]. Again there were rumours of risings and, early in 1801, there were mass meetings in Lancashire and shadowy United Britons were meeting in London. The

Peace of Amiens appears to have defused whatever threat may have existed, though some activists continued to meet and dream of insurrection; it simply was not possible for the government and local authorities to suppress all of the convivial debating clubs which continued to function in alehouses – sometimes unlicensed – in the courts and alleyways of depressed artisan districts [72]. On 16 November 1802, the authorities arrested Colonel Edward Marcus Despard and several others in the Oakley Arms pub in Lambeth. Despard, a former comrade in arms of Nelson, was the youngest member of an Irish landed family. He had been a member of both the LCS and the United Irishmen and was imprisoned under the suspension of the Habeas Corpus Act in 1798. Quite what the extent of Despard's conspiracy was remains a matter of dispute. Marianne Elliott concluded that it was, like Robert Emmet's plot in Ireland some months later, a premature manifestation of a larger, mainly Irish conspiracy which hoped to work in conjunction with a French invasion [64]. For Roger Wells, in contrast, while he acknowledges clear Irish connections, Despard's conspiracy was a serious insurrectionary plot based in London but with United Britons in the north, particularly in Yorkshire, ready to rise when the signal came [82 chapter 11].

Despard and six others, including two guardsmen, were found guilty of treason and executed on 21 February 1803. The insurrectionary threat of the United Britons died with them, though the idea of a revolutionary conspiracy was kept alive in London by the followers of Thomas Spence at least until the pathetic Cato Street Conspiracy of 1820. Radicalism and demands for reform continued throughout the war against Napoleon, but for a time, not least because the conflict with Napoleon appeared unavoidable and defensive, both were muted. Radicalism itself took a variety of forms ranging from the revolutionary agrarian theories of the Spenceans to the political demands voiced in parliament by Sir Francis Burdett. In some districts the Luddite disturbances of 1811–12 suggest evidence of the participants having absorbed radical ideology. Some radicals, like Thomas Hardy, maintained a sympathy for France even under Napoleon. Others saw France swinging back towards tyranny both at home and, especially after the invasion of the Iberian peninsula, abroad. The Friends of Peace continued to press for reform. Following the death of Fox, and with most members of parliament convinced of the necessity of continuing the war against Napoleon, the Friends of Peace stood out more clearly as an independent group expressing disdain for the existing political system and inspired by their fervent moral and religious commitment. In 1812 they mobilised the massive and successful campaigns against the Orders in Council and the East India Company's monopoly of trade with the east. And if the British governments who fought Napoleon continued Pittite policies, they increasingly found themselves under pressure to act against the more extreme forms of corruption and peculation which radicals and reformers exposed. In 1805 Henry Dundas, now elevated to the peerage as Lord Melville, found himself impeached. Four years later the Duke of York, the king's son, was forced to resign as commander-in-chief following a scandal involving his mistress and the sale of commissions. Again the demands for economical reform became linked with political reform. Some little change was introduced, but divisions between radicals and Whigs commonly impeded a united front. Moreover, governments, even that of the Talents, generally enjoying comfortable majorities and the support of George III and, following his incapacity, of the Prince of Wales as Regent, were neither prepared nor able to contemplate a parliamentary reform.

LOYALISM AND XENOPHOBIA

Just as the terms 'radical' and 'reformer' embraced a wide variety of beliefs and activities during the 1790s, so with loyalism; and while a semantic debate here would be largely sterile, it is worth noting that radicals and reformers often considered themselves as 'loyal' to the traditions of the constitution. It was neither irony nor satire which had prompted Richard Price to call his sermon 'On the Love of Our Country' and reformers commonly spoke of themselves as 'patriots'. Loyalism, at the time and subsequently among historians, has been used to encompass all kinds of opposition to reform and to the popular societies. In the early 1790s especially, its more aggressive manifestations united around the war-cry 'Church and King!'

The first 'Church and King' disorders occurred in the neighbourhood of Birmingham in July 1791. The occasion was a decision by reformers to hold a dinner celebrating the anniversary of the storming of the Bastille. The targets of the crowds were dissenting meeting houses and the property of leading Dissenters, in particular that of the scientist, Dr Joseph Priestley. Several elements contributed to the trouble. While Priestley had not attended the Bastille dinner, he numbered himself among the liberal supporters of the Revolution. He had long been involved with intellectual debate on scientific, utilitarian and utopian projects for society as a member, together with Price, of the Bowood Circle and more recently as a leading figure of the Birmingham Lunar Society. In June 1791 he was actively involved in trying to recruit for the liberal Warwickshire Constitutional Society. He had urged the disestablishment of the Anglican Church, most notably in *Familiar Letters addressed to the Inhabitants of the Town of Birmingham*, published in 1790; and he had responded critically to Burke's *Reflections*. His attitude towards the Anglican Church and his support for progressive ideas, especially those espoused by the

French, was sufficient to make him suspect in plebeian eyes in the Birmingham neighbourhood. The situation was aggravated in the days shortly before the dinner by the circulation of a handbill declaring that 'the crown of a certain Great Personage' was becoming too heavy for the head that wore it, and looking forward to the day when the nation would say that 'the peace of slavery was worse than the war of freedom'. It is unclear whether this was the work of an over-enthusiastic reformer or a *provocateur*, but it served as provocation. Moreover, the crowds which carried out the attacks clearly had the prompting and sanction of three local magistrates who themselves disliked Priestley and his ideas. The magistrates were initially present with the rioters at the attacks on Dissenter meeting houses, and promised protection so long as private property was not attacked. But the rioting rapidly got out of hand and continued for three days, until the arrival of cavalry [76]. The Priestley Riots were the most extended occurrence of 'Church and King' violence during the 1790s. They happened before the major manifestations of hostility towards the French Revolution and its supporters within the country. And while they may have encouraged some loyalist gentlemen to think twice before enlisting the support of plebeian allies, violent crowds continued to be a significant element in the loyalism of the decade, and particularly in the 'hunting' of John Thelwall during 1796–97 [81]. The Priestley Riots also foreshadowed other elements of loyalism in the decade, notably the way in which long-standing tensions between Anglicans and Dissenters were taken up and transformed by positions adopted in response to events in France.

Gentlemen reformers in Manchester, organised into a Constitutional Society, also held a Bastille dinner in July 1791. A founder member of the society, the local cotton manufacturer Thomas Walker, was also the town's borough reeve for that year and this may have dissuaded any attack on those attending the dinner. But divisions were sharp in Manchester, where Unitarians had pressed strongly for the repeal of the Test and Corporation Acts, and where rejection of the repeal had led local Anglicans to establish a 'Church and King' dining club as early as March 1790. Walker himself was an Anglican, but his support for the Dissenters, his high profile in the campaign for the abolition of slavery, and his convictions of the need for parliamentary reform made him powerful enemies among the town's old-style Tory elite. In December 1792, when Walker's period as borough reeve was long over, 'Church and King' crowds attacked both his house, where Manchester reformers held their meetings, and the offices of the radical *Manchester Herald*. Walker drove the crowd off by firing guns in the air. As in Birmingham, the crowd appears to have acted with the sanction of local magistrates. The following year there was an attempt to have Walker charged with treason. The case came to court in April 1794, but on the lesser charges of conspiring to overthrow the constitution and to assist a

French invasion. It collapsed when the principal prosecution witness was shown to be completely unreliable and to have been well supplied with gin by loyalists to ensure his testimony [102].

The attacks on Walker's house and the offices of the *Manchester Herald* coincided with the creation of the Manchester Association for Preserving Liberty, Order and Property. This body, which contained many members of the Church and King dining club, met twice weekly in the Bull's Head tavern under the alternate chairmanship of Nathan Crompton, a business as well as a political rival of Walker, and Revd John Griffith, a local magistrate who was alleged to have been present with the crowd attacking Walker's house and who was to become the principal figure behind his prosecution for conspiracy. There were parallel developments in Birmingham where, in December 1792, the Loyal True Blues were established. Among the organisers here were the magistrates accused of complicity with the early stages of the Priestley Riots. The Bull's Head Association and the Loyal True Blues were two examples, and two of the most aggressive and violent examples, of the loyalist associations which mushroomed in the autumn and early winter of 1792.

From the outset the association established by John Reeves at the Crown and Anchor tavern in the Strand in November 1792 hoped to promote similar societies elsewhere in London and the provinces. The movement spread rapidly from London to the west country, then into the midlands, the north and, less successfully, to the east – Norfolk in particular, and especially the Dissenters' stronghold of Norwich, remained resistant. The Reeves associations became the largest political movement in the country with perhaps as many as 2,000 societies [86; 87]. Yet active membership was often small. Reeves's own committee advised:

> that the business of such Societies should be conducted by a Committee, and that the Committee should be small, as better adapted for the dispatch of business; for it should be remembered, that these are not open Societies for talk and debate, but for private consultation and real business. The societies at large need not meet more than once a month, or once in two or three months, to audit the accounts, and to see to the application of money.
>
> (*Association Papers*, London, 1793, p. 7)

This suggests that the associations were never intended to be a mass political movement but rather that local elites were expected to organise with a restricted and selected membership. The original intention of Reeves and his government backers was clearly to galvanise local elites, particularly the magistracy, into action against radicalism.

The committees, and the wider membership, were drawn from men of property. In the rural areas the large landowners, yeomen farmers and Anglican clergy predominated on the committees. In the towns it was merchants, manufacturers, professional men, especially those involved in local politics and, again, the Anglican clergy. But Reeves's call to arms met a much wider response than simply from among the ruling elite. Merchants and tradesmen and the lesser clergy also wished to be considered as loyal, and wanted to differentiate themselves from the lower orders who were seen as envious and gullible, and thus likely to be misled by designing Jacobins. As a consequence, the propaganda which developed from the societies became increasingly directed towards two distinct audiences: the rational, responsible 'middling sort', and the 'vulgar' lower orders who needed to be won away from designing men. Paradoxically, propaganda directed towards the 'vulgar' had the result of advancing the process of mass awareness and participation, something which the Reeves societies had been established to prevent [94].

While many of the Reeves societies became actively involved in circulating loyalist literature to counteract the Painite 'sedition' spread by the radicals, others were content to do little more than petition the king with declarations of loyalty and thanks for the Royal Proclamation of 1 December 1792. Some organised demonstrations in which effigies of Tom Paine were ceremonially paraded and then executed, the proceedings finishing with feasting and drinking at the association's expense. Such demonstrations were designed to be both didactic and entertaining. But there were other loyalists who corresponded with Reeves, urging paternalistic assistance for the poor to take the sting out of radical accusations of the selfishness of the propertied and well-to-do; picking up on the emerging Evangelical movement, they saw the need for a moral reform within society to prevent revolution [*Doc. 12a*]. It was not only in Birmingham and Manchester that witch-hunts were organised against local radicals, nor that the loyalists made connections between Dissent and radicalism. Some societies instigated house-to-house investigations to assess loyalty. Magistrates involved with the associations used their authority to warn publicans that, if they wanted their licences renewed, they should not entertain popular societies on their premises. Booksellers who sold Paine and similar works were threatened with prosecution. Proceedings might be dropped following a public apology, but others felt the full force of the law; and while it is difficult to prove jury selection, it appears that, on occasions, careful selection was made. Most notably the juries which tried the 'Scottish Martyrs' were allegedly recruited from the loyalist Goldsmiths' Hall Association in Edinburgh [10 *p. 96*].

The Reeves societies were at their peak in the winter of 1792–93. Their declarations and the propaganda, which they distributed in the form of pamphlets and broadsheets, reassured the government as the situation with revolutionary France deteriorated into war; more generally they served to encourage and strengthen the forces of conservatism, particularly among the propertied classes. Some societies continued throughout 1793 and into

1794; a few of these appear to have functioned simply as dining clubs, but others continued to investigate and persecute 'Jacobins'. At the end of 1795, in the wake of the attack on George III and the agitation over the Two Bills, Reeves contemplated reviving the movement. There was another wave of petitioning the king though, and as has been noted above [p. 34], the content of these petitions was often mixed; in the event, no significant action was taken to revive the loyalist associations.

The success of the Reeves societies was remarkable. Yet not every manifestation of loyalty in the winter of 1792–93 had such a body behind it. James Gillray seems to have had a shrewd eye for what the public wanted in his political caricatures and he produced 14 between 20 November 1792 and 8 April 1793. Two of these mocked the alarmism of Burke and Reeves; two were equivocal; and ten were explicitly anti-French and/or anti-republican with 'The Zenith of French Glory' constituting one of the most striking of his images [150; *Doc. 29a*]. Plebeian clubs and friendly societies declared their loyalty to Church, King and constitution [86], and by no means all anti-Paine demonstrations depended upon gentry organisation; there were also loyal artisans and labourers fully prepared to organise such activities, drawing on the plebeian tradition of Rough Music [*Doc. 15*]. Subsequent victories against the French provided other opportunities for manifestations of loyalty; sometimes these were orchestrated, but again there appear to have been elements of spontaneity as xenophobic John Bull seized the chance to celebrate the triumphs of his soldiers and sailors over 'Johnny Crapaud'. People who did not illuminate their houses to celebrate a victory had their windows broken, and theatre crowds called enthusiastically for 'God Save the King'. Moreover, in a process which had begun after the American war and which had been boosted by his illness in 1787, George III, although caricatured as a figure of fun, appears to have become increasingly popular and the focus of national loyalty and celebration. This appears to have been part of a shift away from a loyalism which saw itself as supporting king, Church and constitution, and towards a much broader-based support for 'King and Country' which J.E. Cookson has characterised as 'national defence patriotism' [124; and also 18; 52].

Among Reeves's correspondents during the winter of 1792–93 there were some who suggested transforming the associations into military or semi-military bodies to suppress internal disorder [*Doc. 12c*]. A similar point was made by Arthur Young, the celebrated and influential writer on agricultural matters, in *The Example of France a Warning to Britain* (1793). Some historians have tended to see the Volunteer movement which began in 1794 as an extension of the Reeves societies [86; 87; 96], but the reality seems rather more complex.

The Volunteers were part-time soldiers who established themselves in infantry companies (generally in the towns) or Yeomanry Cavalry squadrons (in the countryside) to defend the country, and particularly their home districts against French invasion and internal disorder. There were some continuities in leadership between the Volunteers and the Reeves societies, and the Volunteers often publicly expressed their abhorrence of French principles [*Doc. 19c*]. Nevertheless, far from every loyalist association transformed itself into a Volunteer company. The Volunteer movement was, initially at least, much smaller. Only about 160 infantry companies and cavalry squadrons, with a few small coastal artillery batteries, were established during 1794. Most counties appear to have established Yeomanry Cavalry early on; a few other corps were set up in the East Midlands, Lancashire and Yorkshire where popular radicalism had made its voice heard, but the majority of the first wave of Volunteer units were to be found in those coastal counties most menaced by French invasion or privateer action [124 *pp. 26–7*]. Volunteer numbers grew significantly during 1798; in the four months from April to July they more than doubled from 54,600 to 116,000. This was partly a popular response to the threat of invasion, but even before the threat became manifest, volunteering had begun to be encouraged by the government which was concerned about an army greatly depleted by campaigning in the West Indies. The number of Volunteers continued to grow until the summer of 1800; and this was during a period not notable for any external threat, on the contrary it was while Britain was on the offensive as part of the Second Coalition. Numbers declined over the following year when food shortages contributed to a public order crisis.

Far from being the loyalist associations in arms, the Volunteers were a much more unpredictable instrument than the Reeves societies; a few even appeared suspiciously democratic, making demands for the election of their officers. The associations had been inspired by political attitudes and ideas in the context of the threat from French and Painite principles: sometimes these were general and all-embracing, recognising a need for an element of reform as well as expressing reverence for the existing constitution; sometimes they were fired by fear and hatred of all and any ideas of reform. Individual Volunteers might share either perspective, but they also drew on generations of hostility towards France. Their oaths and pledges might declare hostility to the ideas of designing men, but essentially they were committing themselves to service and possibly sacrifice for their local communities and for the nation as a whole. There were many individual reasons for joining a Volunteer company: it could provide exemption from the ballot for the militia; it could be politic to enlist in a company organised by an employer. Yet enlisting in the Volunteers also implied some recognition of civic duty and responsibility, and some recognition of the need to fight in defence of what a man possessed. Of course, the blessings of living under the constitution as settled in 1688–89 might mean something for men of property and might appear as something to be defended, but this can have had little positive appeal for Volunteers from the lower orders. Rather, the latter appear to have accepted the idea, underscored by propaganda, that the threat from the French implied personal danger to themselves and their families. Significantly some plebeian Volunteers were not prepared to turn out against food rioters in 1800. A group of Volunteers near Wolverhampton, for example, informed a local magistrate of their belief that the high food prices had been caused by greedy speculators. They had enlisted, they explained, 'to protect their King and Constitution and ... they hold such offers sacred; but ... it was never intended by them to give security to the inhuman oppressor, whilst the Poor are starving in the midst of Plenty' [quoted in 127 *p. 106*]. Such sentiments prompted concern among many who, like Lord Clifford in April 1801, lamented the 'unfortunate distinction' detectable in the minds of some Volunteers

> that they have complied with their oath of allegiance when they declare that they will fight for their King and Country against the Common Enemy, but think they have a right to withhold their assistance when called upon to support the Civil Magistrate in the execution of what they disapprove – if Men in arms are permitted to reason on the propriety of the Laws our boasted liberty is at an End. [Quoted in 139 *p. 51*]

The parallel does not appear to have been drawn, but had Clifford and others looked back a mere 20 years, they would have found Volunteers in Ireland forcing changes on the government. During the period of the French Revolution some of the men who had constituted the radical element of those Volunteers combined with others to organise armed insurrection.

THE IRISH EXPERIENCE

Eighteenth-century Ireland was divided ethnically, confessionally and linguistically. There were Anglo-Irish, Scots-Irish and Gaelic-Irish, who respectively were generally Anglican, Dissenter and Catholic. Catholics were in the majority; most of these were Gaelic-speaking peasants living and working on the land, but four-fifths of the land were owned by Protestants, often Anglo-Irish gentry. The Catholic peasantry resented having to pay rents to these men as landlords; they also resented having to pay tithes to the Anglican clergy – the Anglican Church was the established church of the country. Resentment occasionally flared into agrarian outrages in the shape of arson, animal maiming, or violence against representatives of the system. Yet the most significant opposition to the government in Westminster came from the Anglicans and Presbyterians of the Anglo-Irish and Scots-Irish minorities. This opposition focused upon

Westminster's control of Irish trade and the Dublin parliament's lack of legislative autonomy.

During the American war, when British troops were withdrawn from Ireland, Volunteer military corps were organised to oppose a possible French invasion. This Volunteer movement began among the Ulster Presbyterians, though it soon spread elsewhere across the country. The Volunteers were men of property who professed loyalty to George III and showed themselves ready to fight his enemies. But they also considered themselves to be, first and foremost, Irishmen, and they used their organisation and the threat of their military muscle to press for free trade and legislative independence. Their claims were similar to those demanded by the American colonists in the run-up to the war. Wary of another rebellion much closer to home, the government in Westminster conceded free trade in 1779–80 and, in 1782, agreed to the Dublin parliament legislating for Ireland, though agreed Irish bills still had to receive the royal assent.

Legislative independence in Dublin, however, scarcely weakened the influence of the parliament and government in Westminster. There were 300 members of the Dublin parliament; most were placemen of various sorts and less than half owed their seats to the votes of the all-Protestant electorate. The principal executive officers for Ireland, the lord lieutenant and the chief secretary, were both appointed in London and were dependent upon the fate of the government there rather than upon the activities of the Dublin parliament. Their subordinate officers were generally totally loyal to London, and while lords lieutenant and chief secretaries came and went, these administrators remained and ensured continuity.

Reform agitation subsided in Ireland given the apparent success of the Volunteer-led movement. But there were reformers, especially among the Ulster Presbyterians, who recognised how limited the change had been and who continued to argue for real autonomy. Some of these reformers proposed enfranchising Catholics, but here there was sharp debate and division. The radicals, like their counterparts in England and Scotland, were excited by the French Revolution and took encouragement from it. In September 1791 Theobald Wolfe Tone, a young Episcopalian lawyer active among the radicals, published *An Argument on Behalf of the Catholics of Ireland* [*Doc. 4*]. The pamphlet put a powerful case for Catholic enfranchisement and won over many of those Protestant radicals who fretted about union with, and voting rights for, Catholics. In October, Tone and eleven others, mainly prominent Presbyterian merchants, met in Belfast to found the Society of United Irishmen, described by one of its historians as 'the most radical and influential of all the British political clubs generated by the reform euphoria of the early 1790s' [107 *p. 24*].

Initially, the United Irishmen were based in the two principal cities in Ireland, Belfast and Dublin. They drew their membership largely from men in the professions – attorneys, barristers, lawyers, apothecaries – in commerce, and in manufacturing, especially textile production. There were a few landed gentry, notably Archibald Hamilton Rowan, a product of Eton and Cambridge and heir to a large estate in Ulster, and Lord Edward Fitzgerald, son of the Duke of Leinster, cousin of Charles James Fox, a distinguished young soldier who was cashiered in 1792 for participating in a republican banquet in Paris.[1] The society sought parliamentary reform along the lines of, and using similar arguments to, the reformers and radical groups in England. It publicised its aims in similar ways: through sympathetic newspapers, the *Northern Star* in Belfast and the *Press* in Dublin, with pamphlets and handbills, and it encouraged debate and political education by circulating pamphlets like Paine's *Rights of Man* and Tone's *Argument*. But for all these similarities with English reformers and radicals, the United Irishmen wanted reform in the Irish context; this meant shaking off what they regarded as an English yoke, and the best means to this end they believed would come from a union of all Irishmen, irrespective of their religion.

During the 1750s the Catholic Committee had been formed in Dublin as a body to press for the removal of the penal laws which debarred Catholics from public life. The committee had become dormant by the mid-1780s, but it revived again in the early 1790s and a dynamic, radical leadership replaced the conservative prelates who had dominated it formerly. These radicals quickly formed a bond with, and joined, the United Irishmen. They expected that a relaxation in the laws against Catholics in England in 1791 would be extended to Ireland. When their hopes were dashed by the Dublin parliament they organised a Catholic convention at the end of 1792 which brought together elected representatives from all over Ireland and conservative Catholic bishops to petition the parliament at Westminster. Pitt's government responded to the petition with the Catholic Relief Act of 1793 which it pressed on the Dublin parliament, but in so doing it succeeded in aggravating all sides in Ireland. The Catholics were dissatisfied because, although the legislation gave them the right to vote, it did not give them the right to sit in parliament. The Protestants in the Dublin parliament felt that they had been betrayed and humiliated. They feared also that more radical demands would follow and that the link between the United Irishmen and the Catholic Committee presented a threat to the political and social order. Moreover, Protestant anxieties for the security of the political and social order were further excited during 1792–93 by the violence of the Defenders.

1. Lord Edward Fitzgerald did not formally become a member of the United Irishmen until 1796, largely because of pressure from his elder brother. Nevertheless, he publicly supported the society and mixed openly with its leaders.

The Defenders had first appeared in Armagh during the 1780s. There was fierce competition among weavers in the province and militant Protestant groups, Nappach Fleet and the Peep O' Day Boys, intimidated Catholics who they saw as a threat to their livelihood. The Defenders were established to protect these Catholics, but by the early 1790s they were spreading far beyond Armagh and embracing an eclectic ideology which included religious sectarianism, millenarianism, elements of an embryonic nationalism, and admiration for French revolutionary ideas and activism. Early in 1793 the Irish authorities endeavoured to cower the Defenders with a series of prosecutions at the assizes that resulted in 21 death sentences and 37 sentences of transportation. But the needs of the war with France gave the Defenders a new opportunity. As regular troops were withdrawn from Ireland, a Militia Act was passed to make up the resulting deficiencies in internal defence. Implementation of the Act prompted disorder as peasant families protested about the loss of their breadwinners in the ballots. The Defenders took an active role in the rioting in those counties where they were already established, and seized the chance provided by the disorder to spread elsewhere. The Defenders were a sectarian, violent, secret society; the United Irishmen were non-sectarian, radical, constitutional reformers. Yet as early as mid-1792 members of the two organisations had been meeting.

In the context of what had gone before and of what was to follow, 1794 was a relatively peaceful year in Ireland. Yet religious, political, social and economic divisions continued to fester. Protestants worried about a threat from the Catholic majority; loyalists stood firm behind the existing system, while the liberals were torn between action which would lose them support in Britain and action which would lose still more support in Ireland. The Catholic hierarchy, alarmed by what had happened to the Church in France, fretted about the radicalism manifesting itself among many of its flock; it was relatively satisfied with the British government's religious reforms, and was particularly pleased when Pitt's government authorised a grant to establish a Catholic college at Maynooth. The United Irishmen continued to subscribe publicly to constitutional change, though some began to adopt Masonic trappings in the shape of secret oaths and their constitutional aspirations began to yield to more radical ideas. Briefly, the constitutional reformers and the Catholic Committee took heart when the Pitt–Portland coalition led to the appointment of a new lord lieutenant. Earl Fitzwilliam, a Portland Whig, was known for his pro-Catholic and liberal sentiments, and while he was given no authority to make sweeping changes in Ireland, his behaviour on his arrival in Dublin in January 1795 suggested that this was precisely his intention. Fitzwilliam began by removing influential, anti-Catholic administrators like John Beresford, the Commissioner of Revenue and one of the figures principally responsible for distributing patronage in the country. His public announcements implied that full Catholic emancipation was to follow. George III was furious. Pitt believed that Fitzwilliam's viceroyalty had to be terminated quickly, and met no opposition from his coalition partners. Fitzwilliam's departure is commonly seen as the moment which ended any hope of healing old divisions. There was rioting in Dublin on 31 March 1795, the day upon which Lord Camden, his successor, arrived. In May the Dublin parliament rejected a Catholic Relief Bill. Later in the year the Armagh Outrages, an upsurge in feuding between Defenders and Peep O' Day Boys, brought about an alliance between the latter and more well-to-do Protestants and led to the foundation of the fiercely Protestant Orange Order which gloried in the triumphs of William of Orange over the Catholic James II a century earlier. At the same time a new, clandestine United Irish organisation was developing, based on divisions of three dozen men swearing oaths to establish a republican government in an Ireland independent of England. Clandestine the organisation may have been, but the government was never lacking for spies among both the United Irishmen and even the ever active Defenders.

Alarmed by these developments, and by the breaches of the Royal Navy's defences first by Lazare Hoche's ill-fated expedition to Bantry Bay in December 1797 and then by William Tate's *Légion noire,* which succeeded in landing in south Wales two months later, Camden decided that he must nip rebellion in the bud. General Lake was instructed to disarm Ulster which was seen as the heartland of the conspiracy. Lake's coercion of Ulster was ferocious. Some of his Catholic militiamen were themselves suspect, and examples were made among them, but the militiamen showed themselves as violent for the Crown as against. Arguably even more brutal was the Irish Yeomanry. Unlike its English counterpart the Irish Yeomanry, which had been established in 1796, consisted of both cavalry and infantry. It commonly drew its officers from landlords and its other ranks from their tenants and servants. Camden had been worried about creating the Yeomanry, recognising the problems that were likely to arise if it appeared that the government was arming the Protestants against the Catholics. He set out to establish a non-sectarian force, and in some areas of the country, at first, his efforts were successful. Yet, increasingly, Protestants made the Yeomanry their own. Some local units originated in armed groups that had been organised earlier to repel or avenge attacks by Defenders; and in May 1797, while condemning sectarianism in the disarming of Ulster, the government formally permitted bodies of Orangemen to join the Yeomanry.

The disarming of Ulster deprived the United Irishmen in the province of much of its leadership and weaponry. But by forcing fugitives into other provinces it served to spread the organisation still further. And the violence of the action provoked anger and provided martyrs, most notably the young Presbyterian farmer William Orr who was tried and executed on dubious evidence of attempting to swear two soldiers into the society. Moreover if Ulster was, at least partially, disarmed, the United Irishmen were far from finished. The society was already involved in spreading its message among Irishmen in England and Scotland, and early in 1797 it opened new negotiations with the French for assistance. Again, spies kept the Irish administration fully informed of what was happening and on 12 May 1798, as it discussed plans for armed insurrection, the bulk of the society's leadership was arrested in Dublin. A few of the leaders, including Lord Edward Fitzgerald, escaped capture by turning up late for the meeting. Over the next two months, as the authorities searched for the escapees, and as the military rampaged through the land seeking to root out rebellion, Lord Edward made arrangements for the rising. On 20 May he was captured, but as he lay mortally wounded in Dublin's Newgate prison, the rising began.

The 1798 rebellion was a savage and brutal conflict. Often armed only with pikes, the rebels hurled themselves against the government's troops. No quarter was asked or given; civilians were massacred with soldiers. Some Presbyterians turned out with the rebels, but the rebel armies which sprang up across the Irish counties and which rarely co-ordinated with one another, were seen by Protestant loyalists as peasant and Catholic – and invariably they were. The hierarchy of the Catholic Church remained opposed but perhaps as many as 70 of the 1,800 Catholic clergy in the country turned out with the rebels, notably Father John Murphy who led his Boolavogue (Wexford) parishioners into battle. The rebellion was contained and Camden was replaced, at his own suggestion, by a military man. Lord Cornwallis, the new lord lieutenant, sought to moderate the ferocity of the forces under his command and brought an end to the conflict by negotiating clemency for the arrested United Irish leaders when they agreed to a full confession.

The French contributed a post-script to the rebellion. The Directory had made no precise commitment to send an invasion force to Ireland at any time before the rebellion; and, when it came, the best French troops were bound for Egypt. This, however, had not stopped United Irishmen in France from making assertions and promises to their fellows still in Ireland. News of the rebellion convinced the French that they should do something. A tiny Franco-Dutch invasion force was prepared, and three larger forces were assembled in Brest, Dunkirk and Rochefort. A variety of reasons militated against these forces setting off simultaneously. Not the least of these was the rashness of General Humbert who set sail from Rochefort at the beginning of August. At the end of the month he landed at Killala (Connacht) with 1,000 French veterans. Humbert's small army was joined by several bands of rebels. It inflicted a dramatic defeat on a government army at Castlebar – something which appears to have surprised Humbert as much as anyone, and which was probably due to the Irish militia's and Yeomanry's inexperience of regular warfare and exposure to cannon-fire. But Humbert's success could not last as much larger armies under Cornwallis and Lake closed around him. After a token fight at Ballinamuck on 7 September, he surrendered his tiny force; but no surrender was offered, and no quarter was given, to the Irish rebels who fought with him.

Ten days after Humbert's surrender an even smaller force, which had embarked at Dunkirk, landed in Donegal. The majority of this group was Irish, commanded by James Napper Tandy, a Dublin merchant and a leader of the Volunteers during the American war. Tandy considered the situation that he found to be hopeless, and set sail back to France on 18 September. Two days before this the largest of the three expeditions set sail from Brest. A month later it was intercepted and most of the ships were captured by Admiral Sir John Warren off Lough Swilly. Among the French officers taken was Adjutant-General Smith, otherwise Wolfe Tone. Sentenced to death by a Dublin court, Tone chose to avoid the hangman by cutting his own throat.

The rebellion and its aftermath urged Pitt to establish the union, which he did successfully, though not without the need for sizeable patronage disbursed among Irish MPs [112]. It urged him also to attempt the further measures of Catholic emancipation, which eventually forced his resignation. The union failed to solve the problems of Anglo-Irish relations, while the heroes of 1798, soon to be followed by Despard and Emmet, provided martyrs to be romanticised and mythologised by subsequent generations of republican nationalists.

CHAPTER FOUR

WAR

CAUSES AND COURSE

Britain was not among the coalition of kings with whom the French revolutionaries initially went to war in April 1792, yet Britain was to become the paymaster of successive coalitions and the most intractable enemy of revolutionary and, subsequently, of Napoleonic France. Britain became involved in the war partly as a result of traditional political concerns about the balance of power in Europe, but there were also concerns about the new principles being proclaimed by the French. Ideology and strategic considerations became inextricably linked on both sides and while there may be some justification for the historian seeking to assess the significance which can be given to traditional political concerns as opposed to new ideological ones, governments rarely have the time or the inclination to rationalise and compartmentalise such decisions about an impending or a continuing conflict. Moreover, throughout the conflict with revolutionary France, different ministers, while they were united behind Pitt in fighting the war, had different views of the reasons for fighting and different hopes for the outcome [131 *pp. 43–8; Doc. 28*].

During the summer of 1792, under the pressure of the European war, the Revolution took further radical lurches. In Britain, while still neutral, Pitt's government became increasingly concerned about the political principles of the French. French victories in the autumn aggravated these concerns, especially when, in November, the National Convention decreed the opening of the River Scheldt. This threatened the integrity of the Dutch Republic since, while the river largely flowed through Belgian territory now occupied by the French, its mouth opened to the sea on Dutch territory. Britain had long been sensitive about Dutch independence, and as recently as 1788 she had signed a treaty guaranteeing the Republic's internal and external security. Negotiations with the French at this point were impeded by a lack of diplomatic machinery since the British ambassador in Paris had been withdrawn following the storming of the royal palace of the Tuileries in August, and Lord Grenville, the foreign secretary, had refused to accept the credentials of the new French ambassador. The situation was aggravated further when, three days after the Scheldt decree, the Convention promised 'fraternity and assistance to all people who wish to recover their liberty'. Bombast almost certainly outweighed intent in this promise, nevertheless Pitt's government was already anxious about links between the popular societies and the French and there were rumours of French secret agents active in Britain and of plans for insurrection [48; 65; *Doc. 13*].

Throughout December 1792 and January 1793 there was a growing expectation of war. Pitt's government mobilised the county militias and prohibited the export of grain to France; it was convinced that the Royal Navy was well-prepared and superior to any fleet that the French could put to sea. Loyalist publicists and members of the Reeves associations looked forward to war as the surest way of defending Britain against those whom they perceived to be atheists and levellers. The execution of Louis XVI in January increased the sense of outrage over French behaviour. Traditionally, 30 January was the day for a sermon of remembrance to be preached in Westminster Abbey recalling the execution of Charles I. Attendance at the sermon had been thin for years but, in 1793, with the sermon coming just eight days after the execution of Louis XVI, Pitt, Dundas, most of the cabinet, more than 100 MPs and scores of peers attended.

Given the sorry internal state of France, both Pitt's government and the loyalists expected a short war – though the retreat of Frederick the Great's veterans after the battle of Valmy in September, and the over-running of the Austrian Netherlands after the defeat of the Habsburg army at Jemappes in November, should have given them reason to pause. But while British politicians and loyalists were convinced of their own strength and superiority, and of the weakness of their potential enemy, the French interpretation was quite the contrary – their Revolution appeared all-conquering, while Britain appeared feeble. Members of the French National Convention, flattered and misled both by the reports of their ambassador and by the praise of deputations and declarations from the popular radical societies, believed that Britain was on the brink of popular insurrection. Privately, some in the ruling Girondin faction may have preferred some sort of agreement with Pitt, but their public stance, and their inability given their political situation to reconsider the November decrees and to guarantee the security of the Netherlands, effectively militated against any concessions. The French declaration of war on 1 February 1793 seemed to many on both sides to be the inevitable outcome of the increasing tension and hostility, and it probably pre-empted a similar declaration from the British.

It is, of course, one thing to decide to go to war, but rather another to proceed to fight it; and the problem is compounded if the aims of the conflict are confused. It had been British policy during earlier eighteenth-century wars to seek to acquire colonies at the enemy's expense, to keep its own military participation on continental Europe to a minimum, and to hire foreign, usually German, mercenaries. The tradition of a large, powerful navy and a small army favoured such a policy; though it would also be true to say that the policy itself contributed to the shaping of the armed forces. Within Pitt's cabinet, Henry Dundas particularly always saw the war as an opportunity for seizing French overseas possessions. However, if the main aim of the war was to be the extinction of Jacobin principles in Europe, then seizing colonies was irrelevant; the focus of the conflict had to be in Europe, fighting side by side with both other powers and the internal enemies of the Revolution in France. Lord Grenville showed increasing preference for this option and for the restoration of the Bourbon monarchy; Portland and Windham also favoured this option when they entered the cabinet in 1794. Failure to agree on the precise aims of the war meant that, from the outset, there were attempts to pursue all of the options available. Dundas organised expeditions to the Indies. A small army under the command of the Duke of York, George III's son, was dispatched to the Low Countries to assist Dutch and German allies. There were plans to assist counter-revolution in France with troops and with money. German mercenaries were hired and negotiations were begun to subsidise those major German powers who were maintaining armies in the field.

The acquisition of French colonial possessions was relatively successful. The West Indian island of Martinique fell to British forces early in 1794. The island contained a major naval base and, while fighting continued, its loss made it impossible for the French to dispatch and to maintain large fleets that could seriously contest control of the Caribbean with the British for the rest of the decade. British naval superiority elsewhere meant that when the Dutch entered the war on the side of the French in 1795, their overseas possessions also became vulnerable. Both the Cape of Good Hope and Ceylon were seized from the Dutch within a year. But in Europe British arms, and those of Britain's allies, were far less successful.

The attempts to put small forces ashore in France so as to assist counter-revolution were disastrous. A small Anglo-Spanish force landed in Toulon in August 1793, and was forced to withdraw in December. In July 1795 British ships landed a French *émigré* army at Quiberon to assist the insurrection in the west of France. Within a matter of days the expedition was totally crushed. The war in the Low Countries began with some success but by the end of 1793 the French had begun gaining ground. By the end of the following year they had again occupied Belgium and early in 1795 they occupied Holland. The Duke of York's army was forced to retreat in appalling weather; its remnant struggled into North Germany and was picked up by British ships in Bremen in April. An important contribution to

French success was the way that the allied coalition had begun to fall apart internally. The Austrians and, in particular, the Prussians saw more benefit to be gained from a further partition, and final dismemberment, of Poland than from war with France. At the same time there were tensions over money: the Austrians were slow to repay British loans; while in Britain concerns about the internal state of the country early in 1794, and the parliamentary time taken up by the suspension of the Habeas Corpus Act, led to delays in the promised subsidy to Prussia. By the summer of 1795 both Prussia and Spain had made peace with France. Pitt's government offered a subsidy to Russia and a large loan to the Habsburg Empire to bring the former into the war and to keep the latter fighting. The money was accepted, but Poland remained the main interest of both these allies.

Extricating a country from war can be far more difficult than participation in the first place, and Pitt's government was to find this out painfully during 1796 and 1797. There continued to be those who insisted that there should be no peace without the defeat of France and its revolutionary principles. Burke maintained such a position; so too did George III and government ministers like William Windham. Pitt himself disliked war, and particularly its impact on national finances. By the summer of 1796 he was convinced that some attempt needed to be made to bring the conflict to a conclusion, and not merely because of the war's deleterious financial impact. Pitt feared that his remaining allies were unlikely to want to continue fighting for much longer; he suspected, correctly, that the Franco-Dutch alliance was likely soon to be joined by Spain, and that Prussia was preparing an anti-British, armed neutrality on the lines of the one which had been organised in the worst period of the American war. As a consequence, and with the support of foreign secretary Grenville, Pitt persuaded George III to permit a peace mission. In October 1796 Lord Malmesbury travelled to Paris to open discussions.

Malmesbury's mission was complicated by the diplomatic and military events that coincided with it. He left Britain as news of a Spanish declaration of war strengthened the position of the French. At the same time the Habsburg court heard of its armies' successes in Germany, and had growing confidence in its ability to encourage Catherine the Great to bring Russia into the war against France. But by mid-November the French appeared once again to have the strongest hand when news came of the death of Catherine and of new successes by General Bonaparte against the Austrians in Italy. At the same time General Hoche was confidently making the final preparations for his expedition to Ireland, intent on bringing the war home to the British. Hoche sailed on 16 December; and two days later the French ordered Malmesbury to leave Paris.

In July 1797 Malmesbury returned to France. This time the venue was Lille. Again the French had the strongest hand, not the least because

Bonaparte had now forced the Austrians into a preliminary peace. Malmesbury's discussions, which were complicated by intrigues within the French leadership, dragged on until September; but the outcome was the same as before. The war was to continue.

For most of 1798 Britain fought on alone against France. The disappointments of Malmesbury's missions, together with the resolution both of the naval mutinies and the financial crisis of 1797, fostered a new resolve to fight on. The French leadership for its part, seeing the mutinies, the financial problems, and the unrest in Ireland which looked likely to spill over into England, was convinced that Britain was on the point of exhaustion. In December 1797 the young, fabulously successful General Bonaparte was given command of the army of England. Invasion seemed imminent; but it never came. In May 1798 the French fleet and transports gathered in Toulon to set off in pursuit of Bonaparte's chimera, an expedition to Egypt; this, he had convinced his political masters, was the best way to destroy the British and to advance *la grande nation*. The French were narrowly missed by Nelson's fleet as they sailed eastwards, seizing Malta in June. On 1 July they landed in Alexandria; on 21 July they defeated the Mameluke army at the Pyramids, entering Cairo on 24 July. A week later, however, events took a different turn, when Nelson found the French fleet and destroyed it in Aboukir Bay. Nelson's victory was a sensation; his destruction of the French fleet destroyed the idea of French invincibility. Bonaparte and his army were trapped in Egypt; the Royal Navy was master of the Mediterranean; and Britain's old allies saw the chance to settle scores and aggrandise themselves at French expense.

In the closing months of 1798 British ministers and diplomats negotiated urgently with their counterparts in other European courts, seeking to put together and subsidise a second coalition against France. The new coalition, and British war policy, followed paths similar to their predecessors. Initial success in Italy and, to a lesser extent, in Germany was soon turned round by the French. Attempts to encourage and support counter-revolution within France came to nothing. A British army combined with a Russian army to invade Holland at the end of August 1799, and had to be evacuated the following October. By the end of 1800, although Austria was still in the war, Russia was busy organising Denmark, Prussia and Sweden into the League of Armed Neutrality against Britain. In the wider world, however, British arms were more successful. Dutch, Spanish and Swedish possessions were taken in the West Indies. In September 1800 Malta was captured by a British force *en route* for Egypt, and in March 1801 the same army defeated Bonaparte's veterans at Alexandria. Bonaparte himself, of course, had returned to France 18 months earlier, and was now firmly ensconsed as First Consul of the French Republic.

Early in 1800, shortly after his *coup d'état*, Bonaparte had suggested peace negotiations with Britain, only to be rebuffed by Pitt's government. But in March 1801 Pitt was replaced by Henry Addington who, in his first speech to the Commons as prime minister, announced his intention 'to take such steps as appeared ... best calculated for the restoration of peace; [and] that no considerations, arising from the form of government in France would ... obstruct negotiation' [quoted in 60 *p. 118*]. Determined opponents of France and French principles, such as Windham, remained hostile, but Addington was supported by Pitt, by the majority in parliament and also, it would seem, by a war-weary population. Bonaparte also had a war-weary population, and he responded to conciliatory moves offered by Addington by giving wide discretion to Louis-Guillaume Otto, the French diplomat charged with arranging an exchange of prisoners of war. Throughout the summer Otto and Lord Hawkesbury, Addington's foreign secretary, discussed peace terms. On 1 October 1801 the Treaty of London was signed, a preliminary to the Peace of Amiens.

The eventual peace was rather more favourable to France than to Britain, but it reflected the course of the conflict. Britain agreed to surrender all of her conquests with the exception of Ceylon and the former Spanish colony of Trinidad. The French promised to withdraw from central and southern Italy, and to compensate the House of Orange for its expulsion from Holland. If the war had been fought to prevent French hegemony in Europe it had singularly failed; and similarly if it had been fought to destroy the ideas of liberty, equality and fraternity. Pitt supported the peace, and so did the influential military and naval men Cornwallis, Nelson and St Vincent. Some of Pitt's ministers, notably Grenville and Windham, were highly critical; for Windham the treaty was the country's 'death warrant'. Addington himself doubted that it would be possible to live in peace with a Europe dominated by Bonaparte and France. Events were to prove his fears right. Arguments over the implementation of the treaty began when the ink of the signatures was scarcely dry. But it was nevertheless the case that the British people and the British economy were grateful for the respite provided by the Peace of Amiens, brief though it was to prove.

MEN, MONEY, MUNITIONS

Wars require men for the armed services, the men require equipment, munitions, provisions, transport, and both the men and their needs require money. In the revolutionary and Napoleonic wars Britain also committed herself to subsidising allies, both with munitions and with cash; she became the arsenal and the paymaster of a succession of anti-French coalitions. While Britain had fought France on and off throughout the eighteenth century and had developed an effective administrative machine for financing war, the wars which began for her in 1793 were qualitatively and quantitatively different from their predecessors. The French Revolution's early attempts at conscription, coupled with the idea that every citizen should be prepared to lay down his life for his country, meant that more men were available for the battlefield than when armies were simply the professional, paid mercenaries of kings. French generals no longer fought wars of manoeuvre, seeking to seize an enemy's magazines and establish a major tactical advantage before bringing him to bloody and costly battle. The young generals of the Revolution, with the plentiful resources offered by conscription and revolutionary enthusiasm, eagerly sought battle, and, relying on the revolutionary ardour of their men, they aimed at the complete destruction of the enemy. Britain never resorted to conscription, and with a much smaller population (about 10 million as opposed to about 28 million) she could never have matched the French in numbers. But if at times Britain appeared inclined to fight to the last Austrian, Prussian or Russian, it nevertheless remains the case that the wars prompted her to dig deeper than ever before into both her financial and manpower resources.

In 1793 the effective strength of the British regular army was about 45,000 officers and men, of whom roughly two-thirds were serving in garrisons overseas. By 1801 the regular army had risen to some 170,000. These numbers include foreign troops in British pay (though not the subsidised armies of major allies), nevertheless the majority of these men had been recruited in the British Isles with the Irish and above all the Scots disproportionately represented. The Royal Navy on the eve of war had 115 ships of the line, though only a dozen of these were in commission, and there were 16,000 seamen. By the Peace of Amiens 130,000 seamen were manning over a hundred ships of the line and other smaller vessels. Again some of the men were foreign, having been pressed from ships at sea or picked up by the press gangs in British ports. The seizure of American seamen for the British fleet was to become a major bone of contention between Britain and the United States, particularly during the war with Napoleon.

Casualties among servicemen during the 1790s were enormous. This was not due so much to enemy action as to disease, especially in the West Indies. About 89,000 British troops sailed to the Caribbean between 1793 and 1801, and 45,250 died there, particularly as a result of the mosquito-borne diseases of malaria and yellow fever. The casualty figures of one regiment are indicative of the problem. Between 1796 and 1797 the 31st Foot lost 55 men to enemy action and 764 men to disease – in all some 77 per cent of its strength [125 *p. 338*].

Traditional methods were employed for raising men. Army recruiting parties scoured the towns looking for likely lads, and giving the king's shilling and a bounty to those who were tempted or tricked. The dislocation of trade which the war initially occasioned meant that even married men were prepared to take the bounty to tide their families over a period of hardship. In the early stages of the war some civilian recruiters were employed, and sometimes these used methods little short of kidnapping. Stories that such 'crimps' were acting in London caused rioting in the summer of 1794 and again the following year [137]. There were suspicions among the authorities that the LCS was involved in fomenting the disorder, though the proof was never forthcoming. Even before the second wave of trouble non-military personnel were forbidden from recruiting and the police magistrates of the metropolis were charged with investigating recruiting centres.

In the seaports press gangs were active as soon as war loomed and the fleet was directed to ready itself. The gangs were of two kinds: there were those working under the regulating officers, the naval officers permanently stationed in the seaports and charged with recruiting; and there were those which came ashore from warships desperate to make up their crews. Regulating officers commonly sought to reach an understanding with local seamen's leaders and town authorities about how men might be recruited; these officers had, after all, to live permanently in the towns. But often the gangs from warships showed no scruples in their quest for seamen. And it is important to stress that the gangs of both regulating officers and warships generally sought to recruit trained seamen. A man who had served at sea could usually be recognised by the way that he dressed and wore his hair – a pigtail held back by pitch – and also by the walk that he had developed in maintaining his balance on a sailing ship rolling with the waves. 'Landlubbers' could be a liability in a ship until they had learned some necessary skills, and they were only likely to be seized in desperation – though desperation was apparent as the decade wore on.

The men acquired by recruiting parties and press gangs, and the few petty offenders sent into the army or navy directly from the magistrates' courts, were insufficient to meet the demands for men. In 1795 and 1796 the government introduced a series of Quota Acts. These Acts set specific numbers of men to be provided, principally for the navy, by the different counties, towns and seaports. The burden of organising the recruits fell to the local authorities [*Doc. 20*], and there were fines for failure or neglect. The numbers demanded were never reached, especially those delineated in the second set of Acts passed towards the end of 1796. Few trained seamen appear to have been recruited as a result of the Acts, and it has been popular to blame the Acts for introducing into the navy the men who caused the mutinies of 1797. This accusation is probably unfair; many of the quotamen had scarcely reached the fleet when the trouble flared and few of them are likely to have had the ability to sway men who were the veterans of the sea and of battles. What the Acts do appear to have provided, however, are numbers of young men without naval skills but who were subsequently successfully trained for service at sea.

The servicemen discussed in this chapter so far were those recruited for fighting on the seas or overseas; and volunteer corps were discussed earlier in the context of loyalism (see above pp. 44–6). There were also other troops recruited for home defence. Each county in England and Wales had a militia regiment recruited by ballot from able-bodied men aged between 18 and 45. In practice there were many men who, because of status or profession, were exempt from the ballot and it was always possible for a balloted man either to pay a £10 fine, which the county could then put towards the hiring of a substitute, or else to find and hire such a substitute himself. The upshot of the search for substitutes was that militia and army recruiting parties were often chasing the same men. The militia regiments could appear rather more attractive to potential recruits since counties were required to pay a weekly dole of one day's labour at the local rate to the wives of militiamen and any legitimate children under ten years of age. No such payment existed for the wife and children of the regular soldier. Moreover, while the militia regiments were embodied during wartime and looked and served, to all intents and purposes, like regular soldiers, they could not be sent out of the country.

Initially there were no similar militias in Ireland or Scotland. An Irish militia was established in 1793 when it was considered necessary for internal defence, though by it Pitt hoped also to win the loyalty of Catholics now entitled to defend their land in arms. As noted above [see p. 49], the ballots in Ireland provoked serious disorder. When the militia was eventually established, the officers and NCOs appear to have been overwhelmingly Protestant while the militia's rank and file contained large numbers of Catholics, and there were doubts about the latters' loyalty as the fear of insurrection mounted. In Scotland it had been usual to recruit fencibles for home defence; these were regulars who enlisted solely for home service. Considerable numbers of such troops were recruited in the early years of the war, but Dundas was keen to mobilise all available manpower and a Scottish Militia was established in 1797. Many Scots, especially in the arable Lowlands, appear to have thought that being balloted for the militia was the first step to being sent into the regular army and posted to the fever-ridden West Indies. But the riots against balloting for the Scots Militia were short-lived and relatively isolated, even if a confrontation between a crowd and troops at Tranent in August 1797 did result in twelve deaths – one more than at Peterloo [115; 117; 118].

Dundas's hope, shared with Pitt, that it would be possible to have Britain's manpower resources trained for war led to two new departures being introduced alongside the Quota Act of October 1796. A Provisional

Cavalry was established as a kind of horse militia to be balloted from among men who paid the horse tax. At the same time a supplementary militia was created; this was intended to triple the size of the English Militia and ensure that England provided men for the military effort in proportion to her means. The Provisional Cavalry was not a success and was wound up within three years. The implementation of the supplementary militia ballot provoked isolated, brief riots similar to the trouble generated by the Scots Militia; but more seriously, the supplementary militia made it harder than ever for the regular army to find recruits.

In emergencies such as the wave of food riots that swept the country during the period, militiamen were used for internal order. Quartered far from their homes and subject to military discipline they were seen as more dependable in such circumstances than many Volunteer companies, especially the Volunteer urban infantry units. But militiamen spent much of their time in large cantonments on or near the coasts waiting for the invasion that never came. These thousands of trained men were a temptation for the strategists who sought troops for overseas campaigns. In 1798 legislation was passed permitting English militia regiments to volunteer for service in Ireland. But even among the regiments that volunteered there were many men who refused to go and who, in consequence, had to be left behind. In the same year, and again in 1799, concerted efforts were made to encourage men to transfer to the regular army from first the supplementary militia and then, much more successfully, from the militia proper. In 1799, 15,700 militiamen transferred, thus enabling the government to field an army for the ill-fated Anglo-Russian expedition to Holland.

Raising money for the wars was no less difficult than finding men; but while Britain's manpower resources were much more meagre than those of France, her ability successfully to raise money for war was widely admired and envied throughout eighteenth-century Europe. Money was raised both by taxes and loans; large loans can only be negotiated if the recipient's credit is healthy, and successive governments had demonstrated an ability to service the national debt and to pay their dues on time and at promised rates. Between 1665 and 1790 the amount of money which was collected by the exchequer increased fourfold as a share of the national income and sevenfold in real terms.

The taxation system in eighteenth-century Britain was increasingly dominated by indirect taxes. Generally speaking, these did not fall on the necessaries of life such as basic foodstuffs, but on other items of consumption. It was the relatively well-to-do who paid more and more into the exchequer. This was not something which had been deliberately devised as government policy. Governments had proceeded by innovation and trial and error in finding what they could efficiently tax, and what they could convince people to pay. There was widespread evasion, especially in

Scotland, but by eighteenth-century standards the system worked well and was directed by a relatively efficient administrative machine.

Pitt, as emphasised earlier, was a very competent financial administrator. In the aftermath of the disaster of the American War of Independence he restored financial stability to the country and then introduced an imaginative set of expedients designed gradually to pay off the national debt by tax revenues. Unfortunately his plans were derailed by the outbreak of war in 1793, and while he had developed a novel long-term scheme for the country's financial future, he had no new system for raising money to fight a war. For the first five years of the conflict the government followed the usual system of raising loans and tinkering with existing forms of taxation in the annual budget. Between 1793 and 1798 only 11 per cent of the extra revenue came from taxes as new duties were put on such items as wines and spirits, tea, tobacco, various forms of insurance, and hair powder, and as bounties were cut on the sugar and salt trades. The rest of the money came from loans – £11 million announced in the budget for 1794, the special 'Loyalty Loan' of £18 million fully subscribed in 15 hours at the beginning of December 1796, and so on.

The burden of increased taxation drew attention to the fiscal-military state. The Friends of Peace had made little headway in protesting that the war was unjust and that the French had embarked upon it as a war of defence, but their protests about the cost of the war had appeal. This was especially the case in the way that they stressed how increased taxes on farmers, and the suspension of cash payments by the Bank of England, contributed to scarcity. The arguments were pressed on Pitt by his evangelical friend William Wilberforce. In 1797 Pitt established a Finance Committee to preserve some executive initiative over new moves for economical reform. The committee's report fuelled criticism of the system. It noted that the collection of taxes was relatively efficient, but pointed to considerable waste and irregular emoluments [47; 62]. Such revelations gave weight to the criticisms of the Friends of Peace, but the government also faced other, more pressing, fiscal problems.

Within a matter of months of the French declaration of war the financial demands of the conflict had begun to create friction between the government and the Bank of England. The Bank was a private and nominally autonomous corporation governed by directors who acted with reference to their understanding of the country's current and developing financial situation, their responsibility to the government, for whom they acted as banker, and their legal obligation to redeem the Bank's notes and liabilities on demand and in gold. In 1795 and 1796 the directors expressed particular concern about the effect on bullion reserves of the transfer of gold and silver to Europe. Early in the following year the news of Hoche's aborted expedition to Ireland and the actual landing of Tate's small French force in Wales precipitated a run on the banks and a demand for specie. The government responded with an Order in Council of 26 February which relieved the Bank of legally having to redeem notes in gold. The Order was confirmed by the Bank Restriction Act, passed on 3 May as a temporary measure designed to continue until 24 June; in the event Pitt and successive governments renewed the legislation until 1821.

The Order in Council and the Bank Restriction Act technically only applied to the Bank of England, but the country banks in England, Wales and Scotland were compelled to follow suit, and the consequence was a major change in the habits of the nation. People had to get used to conducting economic transactions in paper money, and while there were those who initially voiced serious concerns, the nation settled down to the change very easily and remarkably quickly. Pitt himself, aware of how the preceding four years of war had led to a significant increase in the national debt, and with no immediate end to the conflict in sight, now set out to meet as much as possible of a coming year's expenses in his annual budget. This meant using taxation for a much greater percentage of public expenditure. At the end of 1797 he introduced a bill for trebling the assessed taxes; as usual these were taxes which mainly hit the well-to-do, falling on houses, windows, male servants, horses and carriages. Not surprisingly, given the size of the increase, the measure was unpopular, but as it passed through the commons Henry Addington suggested that anyone who so chose should be able to make their own 'voluntary contribution' to the war effort. Addington's original intention was to provide an alternative to the trebling of the assessed taxes; in the event the voluntary contribution accompanied the tax hike, and it rapidly caught on. George III gave £20,000 from his Privy Purse; Pitt, Addington and Dundas each gave £2,000; at the bottom of the social scale men and women clubbed together and subscribed.

The most controversial and ultimately most productive of Pitt's new taxes was introduced early in 1799, the tax upon incomes. The tax was set at 2 shillings (10p) in the pound for annual incomes of £200 or more. Incomes of less than £60 were exempt, and a graduated scale was introduced for incomes between £60 and £200. Individuals made their own assessments, and swore an oath as to their accuracy. George Tierney, the Foxite MP who had fought a duel with Pitt the previous May, compared the tax to some of the excesses of the French 'in their career of revolutionary rapine'. Again this was a measure which cannot be described as popular. The Friends of Peace saw it as yet another tax falling inequitably and dangerously on the 'middling sort' whose wealth lay in capital and their own hard work, and for whom one unfortunate incident could mean ruin; in contrast, and once again, those with 'permanent property' were being favoured, since they were not asked to contribute in proportion to their property and their ability to pay. In its first year it raised only £7 million instead of the estimated £10 million. But people did their assessments, and the taxes came in. When Addington introduced his first budget five days after the signing of the Peace of Amiens, the income tax was repealed. But his first budget on the resumption of war in 1805 saw the tax reintroduced, with significant innovations.

It is probably an overstatement to describe income tax, as one historian has done, as 'the tax that beat Napoleon' [134 *Chapter* 2]. Nevertheless the introduction of the tax by Pitt, its subsequent development and success, were indicative of Britain's generally efficient system of collecting taxes, and of the preparedness of people of wealth and property to dig deep into their pockets to pay for the war. The problem was Pitt's failure to grapple with the way in which money was distributed and, especially, to prevent peculation. This failure was to provide the Friends of Peace and the radicals with a steady, popular cause through to the end of the war against Napoleon.

FAMINE

Eighteenth-century British governments knew remarkably little about the productive potential of their state. There was no systematic collection and analysis of economic statistics by the board of trade, which was essentially a cabinet committee acting only in an advisory capacity; and the board of agriculture, established by royal charter in 1793 and given a small annual grant, was not a department of government. A succession of disastrous harvests (1794, 1795, 1799 and 1800), together with the wartime disruption of both international trade and internal grain markets, compelled the government to take a positive interest in these issues. It began, admittedly only for a limited time, trading in necessary foodstuffs. More importantly, it was the problem of serious food shortages which focused parliamentary discussion on the census bill of 1800 and which led, in turn, to the first national census being carried out in the following year.

Bread was a major component of the diet of the labouring classes of eighteenth-century Britain. While precise assessments are difficult given variations in wage rates, different family sizes, and the opportunities for women and children in the labour market, it is nevertheless the case that the purchase of bread took a hefty slice from the weekly budget of a labourer's family. Some still consumed non-wheaten cereals – barley, for example, in the west, and oats in the north – but there had been a growth in preference for wheaten bread during the century which was facilitated by improved agricultural methods. What economic historians can demonstrate, but what was unclear to Pitt's government on the eve of the French Revolution, was the fragility of the grain market. There continued to be bounties available for grain export, and imports depended on the state of the annual harvest.

But lacking the necessary figures, the government was unaware that in most years Britain was a net importer of grain. In 1794, 1795, 1799 and 1800 the harvest was seriously deficient. This would have created difficulties in less turbulent times, but in a period of war, and war on an unprecedented scale, the difficulties were aggravated. Furthermore, in a period of political ferment, with revolution across the channel and revolutionary armies as the wartime enemy, the appearance of crowds on the streets demanding bread and 'fair prices' accentuated fears for internal security.

When the deficiencies of the 1794 harvest became apparent, the government felt compelled to intervene by purchasing grain overseas. But this was easier said than done. France was also experiencing shortages and French agents were active in the same markets as British ones in the hunt for grain to purchase. The government was probably aware of the deficiencies sooner in 1799 and on this occasion, since the French harvest was good, there was no competition from that quarter. Indeed, during the second food crisis of the war Pitt's government was even prepared to sanction the purchase of grain from France and her satellites. But throughout these interventions in the market, and especially during the second crisis, ministers were torn between their need to maintain internal tranquillity, especially in London, which meant ensuring that there was sufficient food for the population to purchase, and their increasing adherence to the idea of the free market.

The new notions of the free market originated in the rational thinking of political economists like Adam Smith; and such ideas could easily conflict with the needs and perceptions of the mass of the population. In an analysis of the motivation of eighteenth-century crowds, E.P. Thompson concluded that a considerable number of noisy demonstrations and riots had 'legitimising notions' behind them. The crowds demonstrated and rioted to protect their young men from press gangs and crimps, to preserve their rights to common land, and to ensure access to the necessaries of life. Food rioters in particular – and women were often as significant in these disorders as men – acted to enforce their 'moral economy'. This moral economy enshrined what the popular classes understood as their right to pure food, sold in honest measures at a fair price [139; 140; 142; 143]. Any increase in prices prompted suspicions of profiteering by farmers and middlemen; and millers were commonly suspect for adulterating wheat. The movement of grain in years of poor harvest was resented even in those areas where there was no apparent shortage. Such fears and suspicions prompted crowd action. Crowds marched into markets to fix prices, and then organised the sale of foodstuffs at this 'fair price'. They prevented the movement of grain. They destroyed property, even the valuable grain, of a suspect miller or corn factor; thus, though the crowd might not have it, indeed might not at that moment need it, the profiteer was punished. Such riots generally kept within bounds. They were, as John Bohstedt has argued, 'community politics' wherein the unenfranchised drew the attention of their social superiors to a problem, expecting them to take note and to take the steps necessary to alleviate that problem [139]. In some instances the local authorities responded as the crowds expected, and in 1800 especially such actions brought the ire of the home office where Portland expected that property be defended and the free market be allowed to function.

Any wave of rioting is going to create anxieties for the government. The trouble in 1794–95 was especially worrying for the involvement of troops on the side of the rioters. Moreover, in some instances it was clear that the troops had initiated the disorder. In these years soldiers were sometimes quartered on innkeepers, sometimes housed in the new, often partially-built barracks, and sometimes, particularly in the summer months, established in large camps on or near the coasts. The troops on home duty were expected largely to fend for themselves; many of them were militiamen, who, in many instances at this stage of the war, were neither well disciplined nor well trained. The most serious of the army riots occurred in April 1795 and involved several hundred men from the Oxfordshire Militia. They marched into Newhaven with fixed bayonets where they acquired wheat free from a local magistrate, prevented the movement of flour out of the town, fixed prices on meat, cheese, butter and other foodstuffs, and concluded their efforts with a prolonged drinking session in the town's pubs – they had also fixed the price of beer. The authorities responded with exemplary punishments; two of the Oxfords were shot by firing squad, two were hanged, others were flogged. In the second wave of food rioting, 1799–1801, the troops involved in rioting were generally members of urban Volunteer companies, though it is quite probable that the general dissatisfaction over food prices contributed to unrest among the Guards in London and hence to the involvement of some among them in Despard's conspiracy [82].

In both waves of disorder, but especially in 1799–1801, there were reports of rioters using political language; and some of the threatening letters and notices circulated at the time were couched in a phraseology derived from the French Revolution [*Doc. 27*]. But this raises the question: what meaning should be attached to the use of such language? Obviously it reveals that an awareness of events in France had spread widely. But was such language used as just another lever to bring the gentry and local authorities to an awareness of the problems confronting the labouring classes? Or should it be seen as an element in a more significant shift away from the riot as old-style community or parochial politics to a new kind of activism within which members of the labouring classes looked beyond local boundaries, and which was to emerge in a more tangible shape some thirty years later as Chartism. Both waves of food rioting were linked with opposition to the war. The crowds demonstrating in London when George III opened parliament in October 1795 were reported to have been shouting 'Peace and Bread!' In the second crisis, blame for shortages and the continuance of the war was heaped on the government from a variety of perspectives, and the war and the shortages appear to have become inextricably linked in the minds of many. If the wartime famines contributed to a sharpening of class awareness among plebeian groups, arguably they also contributed to a sharpening of a class awareness towards the poor among what was known as the 'middling sort'. The latter were called upon to furnish taxes for the war and also to pay the increased poor rates necessitated by the militia doles and by the impoverishment of families whose principal breadwinner had been recruited into the army or navy. The famines also led to increases in the poor rates; additionally, those with money were urged to subscribe for the assistance of the poor, such subscriptions being used either to purchase bread or flour which was given away or sold at a reduced price, or else to establish soup kitchens. It was in the midst of these food shortages that a theory was developed on the relationship between population growth and food production which was to have a profound influence on nineteenth-century poor relief.

The Revd Thomas Malthus was the curate of Albury, a parish in rural Surrey; he was also, like others of his rank, a contributor to rising poor rates. The first edition of his *Essay on the Principle of Population* appeared in 1798. It made no reference to the food shortages of 1794–95, but engaged critically, from a conservative perspective, with the ideas of progressive thinkers such as William Godwin, and the French philosopher, the Marquis de Condorcet. In particular Malthus challenged their assumptions about the perfectibility of society, arguing that the tendency of population to increase more rapidly than the means of subsistence would always undermine this. In 1800 he published *An Investigation into the Causes of the Present High Price of Provisions* in which he insisted that the current problems demonstrated the validity of his *Essay*; and a greatly enlarged edition of the *Essay*, published in 1803, made repeated references to the scarcity of 1799–1801. Malthus believed that population growth would either be curbed by the 'preventive' checks of prudence or 'moral' restraint, or else by the 'positive' checks of famine, pestilence and war. He suggested, moreover, that indiscriminate charity served only to encourage population growth. It is easy to appreciate the appeal of such an argument in the context of escalating taxes and poor rates. It is equally easy to see how such arguments could contribute to harsher attitudes towards the poor subsequently enshrined in the New Poor Law of 1834.

Yet there were many others who, during the famines of the revolutionary period, could not leave the poor to the harsh mechanisms described by Malthus. If Malthus was a conservative challenging the prospects for the future improvement of society set out by men like Godwin, other conservatives saw it as their duty – albeit within their own interest – to improve the material and moral conditions of the poor. There was a Christian mission against Jacobinism, epitomised by the work and beliefs of people like Hannah More and William Wilberforce and by the establishment, in December 1796, of the Society for Bettering the Condition and Increasing the Comforts of the Poor (SBCP). The SBCP published and circulated cheap and nutritious recipes and practical information on creating soup kitchens and subsidised village shops. At the same time magistrates, as well as seeking to ensure that there was sufficient bread for the poor in their locality, sought also to ensure a guaranteed minimum weekly income for labouring families. The Speenhamland system, established by the Berkshire magistrates in 1795, was merely the most famous of a variety of similar relief systems set up by county benches during the period to maintain such an income for labourers [22 *esp. pp. 107–21 and 122–3*; 42].

Cold, mechanistic theories of population and the creation of wage allowance systems for labouring families are not the obvious places to look for anti-Jacobinism and conservatism. But anti-Jacobinism and conservatism during the 1790s were sparked by a variety of concerns, and took a variety of different forms and stances.

PART THREE CONCLUSION

Resumption of the war in 1803 was met with resignation. This conflict against Napoleon did not have the same ideological element as that against the Revolution. Rather than joining a confederation of absolutist monarchs to repress a people, the new war had many more of the old elements of fighting to prevent French hegemony in Europe; and such feelings were strengthened first, after the failure of Fox's efforts, as foreign secretary in the Ministry of All the Talents, to negotiate with Napoleon, and then after the French invasion of the Iberian peninsula. The power and relative efficiency of Britain's military-fiscal state enabled her to act as the arsenal and paymaster of the coalitions which, eventually, forced Napoleon's abdication and the restoration of the Bourbons. But, successful though it may have been in weathering the combined impact of the French Revolution and its wars, Britain did not emerge unchanged, and even some of the conservative measures deployed in the struggle served to foster that change.

The Revolution and the ensuing war combined with ideologies and personalities in Britain to produce a new configuration of Whigs and Tories and, subsequently, to foster the interpretation of the Whigs as progressive friends of moderate reform and of Tories as die-hard reactionaries who suppressed reform for 40 years. Such an interpretation has some truth, yet it also hides the complexities of historical change – the disintegration of the old Whig Party, for example, and the emergence of a new Tory Party. Especially, by focusing narrowly on parliamentary reform, it hides the shift in thinking which contributed to the end of the military-fiscal state that had been developing since the wars against Louis XIV.

By the final defeat of Napoleon in 1815, dissatisfaction with the military-fiscal state meant that, once peace was assured, it began to be dismantled. Corruption and peculation had been exposed by the Friends of Peace, by radicals, even by official enquiries. Pitt's disciples in the post-war government were no longer able to justify the big-spending system, but nor were they themselves prepared merely to tinker with a system involving poor auditing, poor command structures, and a high number of profitable sinecures. The men who began to dismantle the war machine and pave the way for the 'cheap government' of mid-Victorian Britain were not Whigs, nor were they new men with a grounding in modern commerce and business. Rather they were the same politicians who had seen the system develop to its most effective in the revolutionary and Napoleonic wars, and whose origins were largely similar to those of their eighteenth-century predecessors [47; 128]. Yet, whatever the dissatisfaction with the system, it is probably also the case that the dismantling of the Hanoverian military-fiscal state was also greatly encouraged by what appeared to be, and ultimately was, the end of the threat of French hegemony in Europe.

While the cost of the war led to dissatisfaction with one aspect of the state, the combined, unprecedented challenge of the French Revolution and war reshaped but strengthened other aspects. Hanoverian England and Wales, and to a rather lesser extent Scotland, were not run by royal appointees seeking to impose the will of the centre. The provinces were administered and governed by the land-holding elite. The local authority of this elite depended on an individual's rank and property; the principal administrative agency through which they ran their counties was the bench of magistrates. Throughout the eighteenth century there was negotiation between the centre and the localities on the running of Hanoverian England; the contrasting lack of negotiation and imposition of Westminster authority led to the initial dissatisfaction within the Irish elite. During the 1790s the gentry rallied behind Pitt's government and while the system changed it avoided any significant moves towards centralisation until the Whig reforms of the 1830s. The number of magistrates increased during the 1790s, and they took on additional wartime burdens; they were responsible, among other things, for militia ballots, for recruiting under the Quota Acts, for organising doles for militiamen's families. Equally, magistrates were charged with rooting out sedition, and with authorising and supervising public meetings. As propertied men they established Reeves societies and Volunteer corps. Above all, the fear of radicalism and its ideas encouraged an overall reassertion of authority by the propertied elite. They stressed the value of hierarchy but, at the same time, they recognised the need to assist the poor both with charitable subscriptions in the time of food shortages and high prices and, more generally, with a better-organised, but still localised, system of poor relief. Hierarchy, paternalism, with a corresponding deference on the part of the poor, and local independence were all stressed as essential elements in a conservative view of English liberty. And urban elites can be seen to have followed a rather similar trajectory, especially in the preparation of home defence. The urban Volunteer corps, established in the mode of a public-spirited, voluntary association, were commanded by local worthies with plebeians making up the rank and file, and they thus were both traditional and provided a model of the hierarchical, respectful society [22; 89; 124 *Chapter 8*].

'Old corruption' in the constitutional system was also exposed and put under pressure by the French Revolution and the wars. Fear of revolutionary consequences of the kind witnessed in France contributed to the check on the ideas presented and debated by radicals and reformers, yet there were changes. In the second half of the 1790s particularly, opposition began to shift away from the monarch and towards the monarch's ministers, who were criticised for waging an unpopular, extremely costly war but who also appeared open to charges of seeking to subvert the constitution to their own ends. George III's reign had been turbulent; in particular there had been the disaster of the American war and his alienation of a group of powerful, political magnates. This had led to the king being the focus of considerable criticism, especially for his choice of ministers. The excitement generated by the French Revolution encouraged debate over the monarchy and its role, yet Marilyn Morris has convincingly argued that reformist criticism and loyalist defence produced a new synthesis of a monarchy which was increasingly demystified and which promised responsible, accessible government [52]. This development was assisted by George III himself. He was hard-working; he appeared the conscientious head of a large family; and his recurrent illness revealed him as both human and subject to human frailties. Caricaturists were not flattering and were often cruel, but from the period of the French Revolution George was increasingly portrayed as a bumbling but essentially well-meaning and patriotic John Bull [16; 51].

If the image of the monarchy was changing, however, the monarch's political power remained formidable; it was not until 1841 that a monarch could be compelled to choose a prime minister as a result of the electorate's choice in a general election, and by then there was a reformed electorate. In spite of the demands of radicals and reformers during the 1790s, the electorate, and the electoral system, remained unchanged. The French Revolution had revived the dormant demands for parliamentary reform; if the French could reform their absolutist system along constitutional lines, it was reasoned, then the British could perfect their existing constitutional system. But while the initial example of the Revolution, coinciding as it did with the centenary of 1688 and with high hopes for the removal of religious barriers in political life, excited British reformers, so the direction which events took in France, especially as war revolutionised the Revolution, agitated conservative minds against any and all change. The conservative voices had the ear and the encouragement of government, and the repression of radicalism followed.

The political repression of the 1790s was sometimes conducted through the courts; sometimes it was violent; and sometimes it was a mixture of threats and warnings, occasionally blatant, occasionally insidious. Such new legislation as was passed by parliament in this context appears to have been little used, though many popular radicals were probably fearful and were thus discouraged from political activism especially in the second half of the decade. The appearance of popular radicalism in the shape of the corresponding societies represents, nevertheless, a significant moment in the development of political consciousness and activism by members of the plebeian order. The creation of the LCS was the starting point for E.P. Thompson in his monumental *The Making of the English Working Class,* and Gwyn Williams, comparing British artisans with French *sans-culottes,* concluded that 'in both Britain and France, it was in 1792 that "the people" entered politics' [84 *p. 4*]. Whether it is safe to pin a precise date to it, there appears a consensus among historians that major developments in the consciousness of what gradually became characterised as 'the working class' can be situated as beginning during the 1790s. There were the radical societies at the beginning of the decade, the economic hardships brought about by food shortages and war, the political and economic repression culminating in the Combination Acts, all of which served to generate a radical consciousness. At the same time there were demands from the state to participate in the war as sailors, soldiers, militiamen and Volunteers. Conservative concerns about internal disorder and the requirements of a war that was being fought on an unprecedented scale meant that appeals had to be made to the working class both to recognise the glories and advantages of the existing constitution and to participate in the war. The more extreme conservatives may have resented having to make such appeals, but there was little alternative. And the focus of loyalist propaganda on the working class, in itself served to generate interest and discussion, and to promote a greater political awareness among that class, together with a recognition of its worth to the state.

Political radicalism with an insurrectionary streak, rebellion in Ireland, mutinies in the fleet and some discontent in the soldiery, together with dislike of an unpopular war and waves of serious food riots have prompted some historians to ask how Britain escaped revolution herself. For Ian R. Christie the answer was to be found in an underlying political and social stability which was based on a relative degree of social cohesion between social groups, on a linguistic and largely Protestant unity, and on a generally expanding and prosperous economy. Roger Wells, in contrast, argues that a very real danger of internal upheaval existed particularly during the years 1799 to 1801 when war and famine led to widespread dissatisfaction, and when English and Scots radicals had developed close links with Irish rebels, providing a potential insurrectionary cadre. Wells is critical of Christie, and others, for losing sight of this crisis in their very broad perspective and time scale. At the same time, the criticism might be levelled at Wells in that he, in turn, loses sight of loyalism and xenophobia [13; 30; 82].

The same period in which E.P. Thompson detected the beginnings of the making of the English working class has also been seen as significant for the development of the middle class. It is tempting to see the Friends of Peace in class terms, at least in as much as they foreshadow the traditional image of the Victorian middle class. They were provincial men, often professionals or linked with developing commerce and industry. They were liberal. As individuals their personal ideology was commonly underpinned by a sincere Christian belief, and most were either Dissenters or Evangelicals. They did not perceive of themselves in class terms, yet Dror Wahrman has shown how, during the 1790s, the term 'middle class' began to be employed primarily by the respectable opposition with reference to the group both best able to ensure political stability and notable as the repository of social virtues. Echoing Thompson's work, he has stressed the significance of the revolutionary period in the formation of the origins of the concept of the middle class. Yet Wahrman's middle class is not so much a social reality as a political ideal encompassing all that was good and dependable within society [57; 58].

In recent years there has been a trend among social historians to shift from the development and distinctions of class development to those of gender. In spite of the appearance of Wollstonecraft's *Vindication of the Rights of Woman* it cannot be argued that the French Revolution contributed significantly to the cause of feminism and women's rights in Britain. Yet it is possible to see the Revolution and subsequent wars as providing some opportunities for middle-class women to broaden their horizons and gain some independence. Women had already participated in the campaign for the abolition of the slave trade in the late 1780s, and some entered the ideological debate on the Revolution, particularly on the literary side, producing both Jacobin and anti-Jacobin novels. On both sides of the debate they commonly adopted an acceptably female mode with their emphasis on education, morality and religion, yet there could be ambiguity here. Hannah More died in 1833 worth £30,000. As Linda Colley has pointed out, she became 'the first British woman ever to make a fortune with her pen, and this fact alone should warn us against seeing her simply as a conservative figure' [18 *pp. 274–5*; 131 *Chapter 7*]. Colley has also stressed how the traditional female virtues of charity, nurture and needlework were enlisted into the public sphere during the war – fund-raising, sewing banners, making warm clothing for troops – an enlistment which demonstrated that the private, female sphere could have an important, useful public role.

Colley has also emphasised the experience of the revolutionary and Napoleonic wars in forming and shaping the identity of Britons, picking up and developing eighteenth-century Francophobia and the notions of the Protestant isle and a people favoured by Providence [18]. Yet there are some qualifications that need to be made. In 1801 Ireland was constitutionally united with the rest of Britain, and the Irish memory of the revolutionary decade and the war with revolutionary France was distinct and different from that of other 'Britons'. J.E. Cookson has suggested that the Irish experience led to a playing down of the role of the Irish warrior, even though Irishmen fought for the Crown in disproportionately high numbers. Moreover, for Protestant Ireland, the experience led to a rejection of ideas for even limited independence. In Scotland, in contrast, the wars prompted a re-invention and a pride in a martial heritage, and as a result helped to foster notions of a genuine equality with England within Britain [124 *esp. Chapters 5 and 6*].

Britain emerged from the revolutionary decade and, subsequently from the Napoleonic wars, as a victor. In contrast with many other states in Europe, Britain avoided the serious internal disruption of revolutionary crowds and/or campaigning armies. With her constitutional system and dynamic economy she looked, in 1815, like a progressive state, though the experience of confronting France and French ideas had reinforced and strengthened some of the old regime elements of an established Church and a localised, largely amateur provincial administrative system. Of course, there were changes, not least in political realignments and the changing views of the monarchy. There was also a legacy in the political ideas debated during the Revolution, and even the conservative ones had, generally unintentionally, helped to broaden and deepen political consciousness across social classes. The French Revolution rekindled debate about political and social reform in Britain, but the radical direction which the Revolution took, and the war, boosted conservatism and reaction. In the short term conservatism triumphed, yet it could only do this by making changes to the structures which it sought to conserve and by appealing, in many different ways, to those whom it sought to keep excluded from the political nation.

PART FOUR DOCUMENTS

1. PRAISE FOR THE FRENCH REVOLUTION
2. BURKE'S *REFLECTIONS*
3. PAINE'S RESPONSE TO BURKE
4. WOLFE TONE ON THE GOVERNMENT OF IRELAND
5. WOLLSTONECRAFT ON THE POSITION OF WOMEN
6. HANNAH MORE'S TRACTS
7. GROWING CONCERNS ABOUT REFORMERS, SPRING 1792
8. RESOLUTIONS OF THE LONDON CORRESPONDING SOCIETY, 2 APRIL 1792
9. A HOSTILE ACCOUNT OF RADICALISM IN SHEFFIELD, JUNE 1792
10. REPORTS OF THE SEPTEMBER MASSACRES
11. LCS ADDRESS TO THE FRENCH NATIONAL CONVENTION
12. LOYALISM AND THE REEVES ASSOCIATIONS
13. THE APPROACH OF WAR
14. SIR WILLIAM ASHHURST'S CHARGE TO THE GRAND JURY OF MIDDLESEX
15. A PAINE BURNING
16. A BOOKSELLER'S APOLOGY
17. WHICH DIRECTION FOR REFORM?, 1794
18. RESPONSES TO THE TREASON TRIAL ACQUITTALS
19. THE VOLUNTEERS
20. ADVERTISEMENT FOR A QUOTAMAN
21. JOHN REEVES ON THE CONSTITUTION
22. SPENCE ON THE END OF OPPRESSION
23. LCS RESOLUTIONS, OCTOBER 1795
24. LOYALIST ATTACKS ON THELWALL'S LECTURES, 1796
25. MANIFESTO OF THE FLEET DELEGATES AT THE NORE TO THEIR FELLOW COUNTRYMEN, JUNE 1797
26. SEAMAN'S OATH DURING THE 1798 MUTINIES
27. THREATENING POSTERS FROM THE FOOD RIOTS
28. GOVERNMENT ATTITUDES TO THE WAR
29. GILLRAY'S CARICATURES

DOCUMENT 1 PRAISE FOR THE FRENCH REVOLUTION

Richard Price was a dissenting minister who had written extensively on political economy. The sermon, from which this is extracted, was preached on 4 November 1798 to the Society for Commemorating the Glorious Revolution of 1688. It became the spur to Burke's Reflections.

I would ... direct you to remember, that though the Revolution [of 1688] was a great work, it was by no means a perfect work; and that all was not then gained which was necessary to put the kingdom in the secure and complete possession of the blessings of liberty. In particular, you should recollect that the toleration then obtained was imperfect. It included only those who could declare their faith in the doctrinal articles of the Church of England...

But the most important instance of the imperfect state in which the Revolution left our constitution, is the INEQUALITY OF OUR REPRESENTATION...

What an eventful period is this! I am thankful that I have lived to it; and I could almost say, *Lord now lettest thy servant depart in peace, for mine eyes have seen thy salvation.* I have lived to see a diffusion of knowledge, which has undermined superstition and error – I have lived to see the rights of men better understood than ever; and nations panting for liberty, which seemed to have lost the idea of it. – I have lived to see THIRTY MILLIONS of people, indignant and resolute, spurning at slavery, and demanding liberty with an irresistible voice; their king led in triumph, and an arbitrary monarch surrendering himself to his subjects. – After sharing in the benefits of one Revolution, I have been spared to witness two other Revolutions, both glorious. – And now methinks, I see the ardour for liberty catching and spreading; a general amendment beginning in human affairs; the dominion of kings changed for the dominion of laws, and the dominion of priests giving way to the dominion of reason and conscience.

Be encouraged all ye friends of freedom, and writers in its defence! The times are auspicious. Your labours have not been in vain. Behold kingdoms, admonished by you, starting from sleep, breaking their fetters, and claiming justice from their oppressors! Behold, the light you have struck out, after setting AMERICA free, reflected to FRANCE, and there kindled into a blaze that lays despotism in ashes, and warms and illuminates EUROPE!

Richard Price, *A Discourse on the Love of our Country*, 1789 (British Library).

DOCUMENT 2 BURKE'S *REFLECTIONS*

Edmund Burke, politician and writer. His Reflections on the Revolution in France *were published in November 1790 prompted by his concerns about the Revolution and about suggestions that the British might have something to learn from it. Burke was, and occasionally still is, accused of inconsistency in that he had supported the revolution in America but, a few years later, opposed that in France. He himself saw no such inconsistency; he set his Whig principles against any increase in royal power and influence and equally against any extension of the franchise and reform of the parliamentary system. For Burke, the best political institutions were a complex system of customs and traditions which had developed across generations. It is largely as a result of the* Reflections, *that he is sometimes accredited with being the father of modern political conservatism.*

You will observe, that from Magna Charta to the Declaration of Right, it has been the uniform policy of our constitution to claim and assert our liberties, as an *entailed inheritance* derived to us from our forefathers, and to be transmitted to our posterity; as an estate specially belonging to the people of this kingdom, without any reference whatever to any other more general prior right. By this means our constitution preserves a unity in so great a diversity of its parts. We have an inheritable crown; an inheritable peerage; and a House of Commons and a people inheriting privileges, franchises, and liberties, from a long line of ancestors.

This policy appears to me to be the result of profound reflection: or rather the happy effect of following nature, which is wisdom without reflection, and above it. A spirit of innovation is generally the result of a selfish temper and confined views. People will not look forward to posterity, who never look backward to their ancestors. Besides, the people of England well know, that the idea of inheritance furnishes a sure principle of conservation and a sure principle of transmission; without at all excluding a principle of improvement. It leaves acquisition free; but it secures what it acquires. ... By a constitutional policy, working after the pattern of nature, we receive, we hold, we transmit our government and our privileges, in the same manner in which we enjoy and transmit our property and our lives. The institutions of policy, the goods of fortune, the gifts of providence, are handed down to us, and from us, in the same course and order. Our political system is placed in a just correspondence and symmetry with the order of the world, and with the mode of existence decreed to a permanent body composed of transitory parts: wherein, by the disposition of a stupendous wisdom, moulding together the great mysterious incorporation of the human race, the whole, at one time, is never old, or middle-aged, or young, but, in a condition of unchangeable constancy, moves on through the varied tenor of perpetual decay, fall, renovation, and progression. Thus, by preserving the method of nature in the conduct of the state, in what we improve, we are never wholly new; in what we retain, we are never wholly obsolete. ...

We are not the converts of Rousseau; we are not the disciples of Voltaire; Helvétius has made no progress amongst us. Atheists are not our preachers; madmen are not our lawgivers. We know that we have made no discoveries, and we think that no discoveries are to be made, in morality; nor many in the great principles of government, nor in the ideas of liberty, which were understood long before we were born, altogether as well as they will be after the grave has heaped its mould upon our presumption. ... We preserve the whole of our feelings still native and entire, unsophisticated by pedantry and infidelity. We have hearts of flesh and blood beating in our bosoms. We fear God; we look up with awe to kings; with affection to parliaments; with duty to magistrates; with reverence to priests; and with respect to nobility. Why? Because when such ideas are brought before our minds, it is natural to be so affected; because all other feelings are false and spurious, and tend to corrupt our minds, to vitiate our primary morals, to render us unfit for rational liberty. ...

Edmund Burke, *Reflections on the Revolution in France*, 1790, [1].

DOCUMENT 3 PAINE'S RESPONSE TO BURKE

Thomas Paine, influential radical pamphleteer whose writings played a significant role in American independence, as well as providing, in the shape of The Rights of Man, *a key text for British popular radicals of the 1790s.* Part One *of* The Rights of Man, *essentially a reply to Burke's* Reflections, *was published in March 1791.* Part Two, *which contained Paine's blueprint for a reform of British society, appeared in February 1792, apparently following a government-inspired attempt to suppress it.*

I am contending for the rights of the *living*, and against their being willed away, and controuled and contracted for, by the manuscript assumed authority of the dead; and Mr. Burke is contending for the authority of the dead over the rights and freedom of the living. There was a time when Kings disposed of their Crowns by will upon their deathbeds, and consigned the people, like beasts of the field, to whatever successor they appointed. This is now so exploded as scarcely to be remembered, and so monstrous as hardly to be believed; but the Parliamentary clauses upon which Mr. Burke builds his political church are of the same nature.

The laws of every country must be analogous to some common principle. In England no parent or master, nor all the authority of Parliament, omnipotent as it has called itself, can bind or controul the personal freedom even of an individual beyond the age of twenty-one years. On what ground of right, then, could the Parliament of 1688, or any other Parliament, bind all posterity for ever? ...

If any generation of men ever possessed the right of dictating the mode by which the world should be governed for ever, it was the first generation that existed; and if that generation did it not, no succeeding generation can show any authority for doing it, nor can set any up. The illuminating and divine principle of the equal rights of man (for it has its origin from the Maker of man) relates, not only to the living individuals, but to generations of men succeeding each other. Every generation is equal in rights to the generation which preceded it, by the same rule that every individual is born equal in rights with his contemporary. ...

Hitherto we have spoken only (and that but in part) of the natural rights of man. We now have to consider the civil rights of man, and to show how the one originates from the other. Man did not enter into society to become worse than he was before, nor to have fewer rights than he had before, but to have those rights better secured. His natural rights are the foundation of all his civil rights. ...

Natural rights are those which appertain to man in right of his existence. Of this kind are all the intellectual rights of acting as an individual for his own comfort and happiness, which are not injurious to the natural rights of others. Civil rights are those which appertain to man in right of his being a member of society. Every civil right has for its foundation some natural right pre-existing in the individual, but to the enjoyment of which his individual power is not, in all cases, sufficiently competent. Of this kind are those related to security and protection. ...

Thomas Paine, *The Rights of Man*, 1791, [7].

DOCUMENT 4 WOLFE TONE ON THE GOVERNMENT OF IRELAND

Theobald Wolfe Tone, Irish patriot. Tone's Appeal *was published in September 1791. Its aim was to convince the Presbyterian reformers in Belfast that their interests were the same as those of Catholic Irishmen and that they faced a common problem – English domination. The aim was largely achieved and, the month following the* Appeal *the Society of United Irishmen was established in Belfast with Tone as a founder member.*

In the following Pamphlet I have omitted all general arguments in favour of a Parliamentary Reform, which equally apply to England and Ireland ... for, after PAINE, who shall, or who need, to be heard on the subject? ...

What is our Government [in Ireland]? It is a phenomenon in politics, contravening all received and established opinions. It is a Government derived from another country, whose interest, so far from being the same with that of the people, directly crosses it at right angles. Does any man think our rulers here recommend themselves to their creators in England, by promoting the interest of Ireland, when it can in the most remote degree interfere with the commerce of Great Britain? But how is this foreign Government maintained? Look to your calendar, to your pension list, to your concordatum, and you will find the answer written in *letters of gold*. This unnatural influence must be supported by profligate means, and hence corruption is the only medium of Government in Ireland. The people are utterly disregarded and defied. Divided and distracted as they are, and distrustful of each other, they fall an easy prey to English rulers, or their Irish subalterns. The fear of danger is removed from Administration by our internal weakness, and the sense of shame speedily follows it. Hence it is, that we see Peculation protected, Venality avowed, the Peerage prostituted, the Commons corrupted. We see all this at the very hour, when everywhere but in Ireland Reform is going forward, and levelling ancient abuses in the dust. Why are these things so? Because Ireland is struck with a political paralysis, that has withered her strength, and crushed her spirit. She is not half alive; one side is scarce animated, the other is dead; she has by her own law, as it were, amputated her right hand; she has outrun the Gospel precept, and cast her right eye into the fire, even before it has offended her. Religious intolerance and political bigotry ... bind the living Protestant to the dead and half corrupted Catholic, and beneath the putrid mass, even the embryo of effort is stifled. When the nation is thus circumstanced, it is not to be wondered at, if even an administration of boobies and blockheads presume to insult and pillage, and contemn, and defy her. ...

... if all barriers between the two religions were beaten down, so far as civil matters are concerned, if the odious distinction of Protestant and Presbyterian, and Catholic, were abolished, and the three great sects blended together, under the common and sacred title of Irishman, what interest could a Catholic member of Parliament have, distinct from his Protestant brother sitting on the same bench, exercising the same function, bound by the same ties? Would liberty be less dear to him, justice less sacred, property less valuable, infamy less dreadful? ...

Wolfe Tone, *An Argument on Behalf of the Catholics of Ireland*, 1791 (British Library).

DOCUMENT 5 WOLLSTONECRAFT ON THE POSITION OF WOMEN

Mary Wollstonecraft began life as a governess. Between 1793 and 1795 she lived in France with the American Gilbert Imlay, with whom she had a child. She married William Godwin in 1797, dying after the birth of their daughter, Mary, who was to become the wife of the poet Shelley.

In the government of the physical world it is observable that the female in point of strength is, in general, inferior to the male. This is the law of nature; and it does not appear to be suspended or abrogated in favour of woman. A degree of physical superiority cannot, therefore, be denied – and it is a noble prerogative! But not content with this natural pre-eminence, men endeavour to sink us still lower, merely to render us alluring objects for a moment; and women, intoxicated by the adoration which men, under the influence of their senses, pay them, do not seek to obtain a durable interest in their hearts, or to become the friends of the fellow creatures who find amusement in their society. ...

My own sex, I hope, will excuse me, if I treat them like rational creatures, instead of flattering their fascinating graces, and viewing them as if they were in a state of perpetual childhood, unable to stand alone. I earnestly wish to point out in what true dignity and human happiness consists – I wish to persuade women to endeavour to acquire strength, both of mind and body, and to convince them that the soft phrases, susceptibility of heart, delicacy of sentiment, and refinement of taste, are almost synonymous with epithets of weakness, and that those beings who are only the objects of pity and that kind of love, which has been termed its sister, will soon become objects of contempt.

Dismissing then those pretty feminine phrases, which the men condescendingly use to soften our slavish dependence, and despising that weak elegancy of mind, exquisite sensibility, and sweet docility of manners, supposed to be the sexual characteristics of the weaker vessel, I wish to shew that elegance is inferior to virtue, that the first object of laudable ambition is to obtain a character as a human being, regardless of distinction of sex; and that secondary views should be brought to this simple touchstone....

To render mankind more virtuous, and happier of course, both sexes must act from the same principle; but how can that be expected when only one is allowed to see the reasonableness of it? To render the social compact truly equitable, and in order to spread those enlightening principles, which alone can meliorate the fate of men, women must be allowed to found their virtue on knowledge, which is scarcely possible unless they be educated by the same pursuits as men. ...

Mary Wollstonecraft, *A Vindication of the Rights of Woman*, 1792, [9].

DOCUMENT 6 HANNAH MORE'S TRACTS

Hannah More was the most celebrated woman Evangelical author of her day. Village Politics *was a response to Paine, first published in 1792, aimed at a plebeian audience, and running through several subsequent editions. It was written as a dialogue between two villagers, Jack Anvil, the blacksmith, and Tom Hod, the mason.* Tawney Rachel *was one of her Cheap Repository Tracts. It told the story of Tawney Rachel, the wife of 'poaching Giles', whose whole family maintained themselves by pilfering. Rachel sold laces, cabbage nets and chap books, and also told fortunes. At the conclusion of the story, Giles loses his life in stealing a net from a garden, and Rachel is transported to Botany Bay for theft.*

(a) Village Politics.
Tom. ... I want freedom and happiness, the same as they have got in France.

Jack. What, Tom, we imitate them? We follow the French! Why they only begun all this mischief at first, in order to be just what we are already. Why I'd sooner go to the Negers to get learning, or to the Turks to get religion, than to the French for freedom and happiness.

Tom. What do you mean by that? ar'n't the French free?

Jack. Free, Tom! ay, free with a witness. They are so free, that there's nobody safe. They make free to rob when they will, and kill whom they will. If they don't like a man's looks, they make free to hang him without judge or jury, and the next lamp-post does for the gallows; so then they call themselves free, therefore you see they have no law left to condemn them, and no king to take them up and hang them for it.

Tom. Ah, but, Jack, didn't their KING formerly hang people for nothing too? and besides, were'n't they all papists before the Revolution?

Jack. Why, true enough, they had but a poor sort of religion; but bad is better than none, Tom. And so was the government bad enough too, as long as they would, and never say, with your leave, or by your leave, Gentlemen of the Jury. But what's all that to us?

Tom. To us! Why, don't our governors put many of our poor folks in prison against their will? What are the jails for? Down with the jails, I say: all men should be free.

Jack. Harkee, Tom, a few rogues in prison keep the rest in order, and then honest men go about their business in safety, afraid of nobody; that's the way to be free. And let me tell thee, Tom, thou and I are tried by our peers as much as a lord is. Why, the *king* can't send me to prison if I do no harm, and if I do, there's reason good why I should go there. I may go to law with Sir John at the great castle yonder, and he no more dares lift his little finger against me than if I were his equal. A lord is hanged for a hanging matter, as thou or I shou'd be; and if it be any comfort to thee, I myself remember a peer of the realm being hanged for killing his man, just the same as the man would be for killing *him*.

Hannah More, *Village Politics. Addressed to All the Mechanics, Journeymen and Day Labourers in Great Britian. By Will Chip, A Country Carpenter*, 1792 (British Library).

(b) The conclusion to Tawney Rachel.

I have thought it my duty to print this little history as a kind of warning to all you young men and maidens not to have any thing to say to CHEATS, IMPOSTERS, CUNNING-WOMEN, FORTUNE TELLERS, CONJURERS, and INTERPRETERS OF DREAMS. – Listen to me, your true friend, when I assure you that God never reveals to weak and wicked women those secret designs of his Providence, which no human wisdom is able to foresee. To consult these false oracles is not only foolish, but sinful, It is foolish, because they are themselves as ignorant as those whom they pretend to teach, and it is sinful, because it is prying into the futurity which God, as kindly as wisely, hides from men. God indeed *orders* all things; but when you have a mind to do a foolish thing, do not fancy you are *fated* to do it. This is tempting Providence, and not trusting him. It is indeed, 'charging God with folly'. Prudence is his gift, and you obey him better when you make use of prudence under the direction of prayer, than when you madly run into ruin, and think you are only submitting to your fate. Never fancy that you are compelled to undo yourself. Never believe that God conceals his will from a sober Christian who obeys his laws, and reveals it to a vagabond Gipsy, who runs up and down breaking the laws, both of God and man. King Saul never consulted the witch till he had left off serving God. The Bible will direct us what to do better than any conjuror, and no days are unlucky but those which we make so by our own vanity, folly, and sin.

Hannah More, *Tawney Rachel or the Fortune-Teller with some account of Dreams, Omens and Conjurors*, 1797 (British Library).

DOCUMENT 7 GROWING CONCERNS ABOUT REFORMERS, SPRING 1792

Lord Auckland (1744–1814), a friend of Pitt who served in a variety of governments, writing to Lord Grenville, the foreign secretary, 14 March 1792.

Though the French wretchedness seems to increase more rapidly than the utmost malignancy of national hostility could ever have wished, I confess myself anxious to see their fate brought to a period one way or the other. The extravagance and profligacy of their doctrines have not yet infected us materially; but I dread them as I would the plague in my neighbourhood, and think it within a reasonable probability that I may live to see all Europe in a state of frenzy and ferocity tending fast to the ancient barbarism. I hope that this is a gloomy and exaggerated speculation; but great and unwearied vigilance is necessary. Many of the present habits and usages of English society, and much of the Parliamentary language and measures, appear to me to be calculated for the levelling system. ...

Nor would it be difficult to show that many of the doctrines bringing forwards in this country, under cover of the slave question and of religious toleration, are in unison with those *des vainqueurs de la Bastille.*

Historical Manuscripts Commission, 14th Report. The Manuscripts of J.B. Fortescue. Preserved at Dropmore, vol. 3, pp. 262–3.

DOCUMENT 8 RESOLUTIONS OF THE LONDON CORRESPONDING SOCIETY, 2 APRIL 1792

Resolved, – That every individual has a Right to Share in the Government of that Society of which he is a Member – unless incapacitated.
Resolved, – That nothing but Non-age, Privation of Reason, or an Offence against the general Rules of Society, can incapacitate him.
Resolved, – That it is no less the *Right* than the *Duty* of every Citizen to keep a watchful Eye on the Government of his Country, that the Laws by being multiplied do not degenerate into *Oppression*; and that those who are entrusted with the Government, do not substitute *Private Interest* for *Public Advantage.*
Resolved, – That the People of Great Britain are not *effectually* represented in Parliament.
Resolved, – That in Consequence of a *partial*, *unequal*, and therefore *inadequate Representation*, together with the *corrupt* Method in which Representatives are elected; *oppressive Taxes*, *unjust Laws*, *restrictions of Liberty*, and *wasting of the Public Money*, have ensued.

Resolved, – That the only Remedy to those Evils, is a fair, equal, and impartial Representation of the People in Parliament.
Resolved, – That a fair, equal, and impartial Representation can never take Place until all *partial Privileges* are abolished.
Resolved, – That this Society do express their *Abhorrence* of Tumult and Violence, and that, as they aim at Reform, not Anarchy, Reason, Firmness, and Unanimity, are the only Arms they themselves will employ, or persuade their Fellow-Citizens to exert, against *Abuse of Power*.

Ordered, – That the Secretary of this Society do transmit a Copy of the above to the Societies for Constitutional Information, established in *London*, *Sheffield*, and *Manchester*.

By Order of the Committee,
T. HARDY, Secretary

April 2, 1792

Thale, [8], p. 10.

DOCUMENT 9 A HOSTILE ACCOUNT OF RADICALISM IN SHEFFIELD, JUNE 1792

Colonel Oliver De Lancey, the Barrackmaster General, travelled through the north of England in the early summer of 1792 and reported on his perceptions of the state of the country.

[In Sheffield] I found that the seditious doctrines of Paine and the factious people who are endeavouring to disturb the peace of the country, had extended to a degree very much beyond my conception; and indeed they seem with great judgement to have chosen this as the centre of all their seditious machinations, for the manufacturers of this town are of a nature to require so little capital to carry them on, that a man with a very small sum of money can employ two, three or four men: and this being generally the case, there are not in this, as in other great towns, any number of sufficient weight who could by their influence, or the number of their dependants, act with any effect in case of a disturbance. And as the wages given to the journeymen are very high, it is pretty generally the practice for them to work for three days, in which they earn sufficient to enable them to drink and riot for the rest of the week, consequently no place can be more fit for seditious purposes.

The mode they have adopted for spreading their licentious principles has been by forming Associations on terms suited to the circumstances of the lowest mechanics, of whom about 2,500 are enrolled in the principal Society, and that it may not be confined, they allow any man to be present who will pay 6d. for admission. Here they read the most violent publications, and comment on them, as well as on their correspondence not only with the dependent Societies in the towns and villages in the vicinity, but with those established in other parts of the kingdom. ...

Public Record Office [hereafter PRO] H.O. 42.20, De Lancey to the secretary at war (?), 13 June 1792.

DOCUMENT 10 REPORTS OF THE SEPTEMBER MASSACRES

From 2 to 6 September 1792 over 1,000 inmates of the Paris prisons were massacred. The killings were sparked off by fears that the approaching armies of Austrians, Prussians and French émigrés *were somehow going to be aided by royalist sympathisers in the prisons – a few of whom were priests who had refused the civic oath and Swiss officers captured when the monarchy was overthrown on 10 August. Most of the newspaper reports in England were condemnatory, like that from* The Times *(a), but the radical* Manchester Herald *published a special one-page edition putting an alternative slant (b).*

(a)
The following report of the massacre on Sunday, has been made by a Member of the National Assembly. Although we know that this report does not state the whole of the facts, which for obvious reasons are concealed, it is however, a very proper article to be here inserted ...

'The Commission assembled during the suspension of the night sitting, being informed by several citizens, that the people were continuing to rush in great numbers towards the different prisons, and were there exercising their vengeance, thought it necessary to write to the Council General of the Community, to learn officially the true state of things. The Community sent back word, that they had ordered a deputation to render an account to the commission of what had happened. At two o'clock the deputation, consisting of Mess. Tallien, Tronchon, and Cuirate, was introduced into the hall of the Assembly. M. Tronchon then said, that the greater part of the prisons were empty; that about four hundred prisoners were massacred. ...

M. Tallien added, that when he went to the Abbaye, the people were demanding the registers from the keeper; that the prisoners confined on account of crimes imputed to them on the 10th of August, and those confined for forging assignats [paper money] were almost all butchered, and that only eleven of them were saved. ...'

(Read this ye ENGLISHMEN, with attention, and ardently pray your happy Constitution may never be outraged by the despotic tyranny of Equalization.)

The Times, 10 September 1792.

(b)

Manchester, 10th September, 1792.

The Editors of the MANCHESTER HERALD, having received some Original Communications from their correspondents relating to the summary punishment of the aristocratic criminals, and the refractory priests, at Paris, on the 2d instant, think it their duty to lay them before the public as speedily as may be, without waiting their regular insertion in the paper of Saturday next. There is no doubt but more than usual industry will be exerted by the enemies of freedom, to exaggerate and misrepresent the important events of that day; events, however melancholy, yet absolutely necessary to the safety of France, and the liberties of mankind. The persons thus put to death, if guilty, obviously deserved the fate they have met with, far more than the more daring enemies of their country, who villainously but openly butchered their fellow citizens in the field. If these instruments of open hostility might reasonably be put to death if taken in arms against their country, how much more the base and hypocritical assassins of liberty, who aim the dagger while they profess to hold out the right hand of friendship, and seek for safety, and obtain commiseration from the weak-minded and moderate, in consequence of the very deepness and complication of their iniquity. That the persons thus executed were guilty, there is very little doubt; and the people at Paris were evidently satisfied that they were so. Of the major part of them (the Swiss officers, and the refractory priests) no doubt whatever can be entertained. Had the times been peaceable, and the regular course of justice possible upon so many delinquents, they certainly ought to have undergone a formal trial, and have been convicted or acquitted, executed or dismissed, in the usual way. But when Paris itself was threatened with a siege, and with all the Horrors of the most savage cruelty, and the most unrelenting vengeance – when the instances of ferocious barbarity among the enemies of France, towards the devoted victims of the rights of Man were perpetual – when no time remained for any thing but self defence, and the formal processes of established tribunals were impossible – what were the people to do? Substantial Justice – and they have done it. We have no hesitation in declaring, that in our opinion, it will eventually prove the truest mercy; and we sincerely hope, it may prove an extensive and salutary warning.

PRO H.O. 42.21.

DOCUMENT 11 LCS ADDRESS TO THE FRENCH NATIONAL CONVENTION

Degraded by an oppressive system of inquisition, the insensible, but continual encroachments of which have deprived this nation of its boasted liberty, and reduced it almost to that abject state of slavery from which you have so gloriously emancipated yourselves, five thousand English citizens, fired with indignation, have the courage to step forward to rescue their country from that opprobrium which has been thrown upon it by the base conduct of those who are invested with power. They think it the duty of true Britons to support and assist with all their might the defenders of the Rights of Man, the propagators of human happiness, and to swear eternal friendship to a nation who pursues the plan which you have adopted; may that friendship be from this day consecrated between us, may the most exemplary vengeance fall upon the head of that man who shall attempt to dissolve it!

Frenchmen, our number will appear very small when compared with the rest of the nation: but know, that it increases every day: and if the terrible and continually elevated arm of authority overawe the timid; if falsehoods every moment dispersed with so much industry, mislead the credulous; and if the public intimacy of the Court with Frenchmen, avowed traitors to their country, hurry away the ambitions and unthinking, we can assure you, Freemen and Friends, that knowledge makes rapid progress among us; that curiosity has taken possession of the minds of the public, that the reign of ignorance, inseparable from that of despotism, is vanishing; and that at present all men ask each other – What is Liberty? What are our rights? Frenchmen you are already free, but the Britons are preparing to be so.

London Chronicle, 12 November 1792.

DOCUMENT 12 LOYALISM AND THE REEVES ASSOCIATIONS

The following extracts are taken from the records of the Reeves Association in London. They have been selected to illustrate different ideas within Loyalism which blossomed across the country at the close of 1792.

(a) *Extract from a letter to the Reeves Association from the Revd R.B. Nicholls, Dean of Middleham, Yorks, 30 November 1792. Nicholls had been in Philadelphia at the outbreak of the American War of Independence and, elsewhere in the letter, draws parallels with the situation in the Britain in which he is writing.*

In vain, Sir, do we look to the writings of Tom Paine or any other Incendiary as the causes of these disorders and discontents we have so much reason to dread among the people, events of every sort are, as one observed, but the exemplification of pre-existent causes. An incendiary may hold the match like Cataline; but the causes of a combustion exist in the moral profligacy and want of religious principle in the bulk of the people; in the little care or attention of the higher orders to the good government, relief and employment of the lower. We must therefore endeavour to change the state of things by making marriage, which is the best political bond, and subsistence easier to the lower ranks, by cutting off as much as possible the sources of corruption, by providing employment for them and promoting religion among them.

British Library, Loyalist Association Papers, Additional MSS 16919, fol. 150.

(b) *Extract from a letter to the Reeves Association from the Revd W.L. Fancourt, curate of Wellingborough, 30 November 1792.*

It has been my endeavour always to instil into the minds of my Parishioners the Blessings of Content, the Love of order, and the Duties of Loyalty – and happy should I account myself, was it in my power to say, that my endeavours had been seconded by my dissenting Brethren. But so far from this that they are daily filling the minds of the people, especially of the lower order, with all the various and pernicious doctrines of discontent. For two years have I observed their secret and indirect methods of alienating the minds of His Majesty's subjects from their duty and interest. But now they no longer take care to conceal their intentions, they speak openly both at their own houses and at public places. Payne's mischievous Pamphlets are distributed about at sixpence apiece; and the justice of his reasonings are enforced by the following methods; to the lower classes of people the inadequacy of wages is urged as a grievance; to the middling orders of tradesmen the Right of Equality with their wealthier neighbours; and to all, the heavy burden of taxes; and if any of the dissenters, the higher class I mean, happen to fall into company with any of the inferior clergy, they by plausible speeches set forth the injustice, as they stile [sic] it, of the large revenues of the dignitaries of the Church, and the small stipend and laborious offices of the lower orders. ...

British Library, Loyalist Association Papers, Additional MSS 16919, fol. 158.

(c) *Extract from a letter to the Reeves Association from Sir H. Tempest, Bt. Hope End, near Ledbury, Herefordshire, 7 December 1792.*

[Your society should consider] a general association in every county, publickly declaring their sentiments and determination to venture their lives and property in defence of the present establishment in *Church and State*. And that a certain number of gentlemen farmers and freeholders, the most able and active in each County should undertake to come forward as volunteers, at a moment's warning, and at their own expense, to do and act under the Civil Magistrate, whatever shall be requisite to support the government (should such exertions eventually become necessary).

British Library, Loyalist Association Papers, Additional MSS 16921, fols 50–1.

DOCUMENT 13 THE APPROACH OF WAR

The following are extracts from a letter written by Lord Grenville, the foreign secretary, in reply to a letter from Monsieur Chauvelin, the French government's representative in London. Chauvelin, whose position was not recognised by the British government, had written earlier to explain the opening of the river Scheldt (16 November), the Decree of Fraternity (19 November), and giving a French promise not to attack the Dutch Republic as long as it remained neutral.

Whitehall, Dec. 31st. 1792
I have received, Sir, from you a note, in which stiling [sic] yourself Minister Plenipotentiary of France, you communicate to me ... the instructions which you state to have received yourself from the Executive Council of the French Republic. You are not ignorant, that since the unhappy events of the 10th of August last, the King has thought proper to suspend all official communications with France. ... I am therefore to inform you, Sir, in express and formal terms, that I acknowledge you in no other public character than that of Minister from his Most Christian Majesty [Louis XVI], and that consequently you cannot be admitted to treat with the King's Ministers, in the quality and under the form stated in your note. ...

[Regarding] the decree of the National Convention of the 19th November, in the expressions of which, all England saw the formal declaration of a design to extend universally the new principles of government adopted in France, and to encourage disorder and revolt in all countries, even in those which are neutral. If this interpretation, which you represent as injurious to the Convention, could admit of any doubt, it is but too well justified by the conduct of the Convention itself: and the application of these principles to the King's dominions has been shewn unequivocally, by the public reception given to the promoters of sedition in this country, and by the speeches made to them precisely at the time of this decree, and since on several different occasions. ...

The declaration which you ... make, that France will not attack Holland so long as that power shall observe an exact neutrality, is conceived nearly in the same terms that you was charged to make ... in the month of June last. Since that first declaration was made, an officer, stating himself to be employed in the service of France, has openly violated the territory and the neutrality of the [Dutch] Republic, in going up the Scheldt to attack the citadel of Antwerp, notwithstanding the determination of the government not to grant this passage and the formal protest by which they opposed it. ...

France can have no right to annul the stipulations relative to the Scheldt, unless she has also the right to set aside equally all the other treaties between all the powers of Europe, and all the other rights of England, or of her allies. ...

England will never consent that France shall arrogate the power of annulling at her pleasure, and under the pretence of a pretended natural right, of which she makes herself the only judge, the political system of Europe, established by solemn treaties, and guaranteed by the consent of all the powers. This government, adhering to the maxims which it has followed for more than a century, will also never see with indifference, that France shall make herself, either directly or indirectly, sovereign of the Low Countries, or general arbitress of the rights and liberties of Europe. ...

A Collection of State Papers Relative to the War against France, vol. 1, London, 1794, pp. 227–30.

DOCUMENT 14 SIR WILLIAM ASHHURST'S CHARGE TO THE GRAND JURY OF MIDDLESEX

Ashhurst's Charge to the Grand Jury was very popular with the Reeves societies. Copies of it were printed and circulated by these societies and other loyalist groups; it was even translated into Welsh.

There is no Country where the Law is more uprightly or more impartially administered. For this blessing we are indebted to the wise and prudent form of our Constitution, and to the security which naturally results from it. Hence it is that our Commerce has been extended beyond the example of all former ages. And we all know that this is the case of every Manufacturing Town in this Country. Such is the flourishing state of this Kingdom, and such the happy Fruits of Liberty and Peace, one would suppose there was not a man in the Kingdom who did not feel it, and feel it with a grateful heart; and yet, I am sorry to say, there are men of dark and gloomy hearts, who would wish to overturn the general fabric of our Constitution, which has been the work of Ages, and would give us in return a system of universal Anarchy and Confusion. There have been Publications in which the Authors disclaim any idea of Subordination, as inconsistent with the natural rights and equality of man, and recommend the example of a neighbouring Nation as a model for our imitation. Alas! Humanity is called upon to pity the deplorable situation of that Country: but it is a very ill chosen example to hold forth to a Nation in a most flourishing state of happiness; and it is pretty extraordinary, that, with our eyes open, we should wish to plunge ourselves into the same abyss of misery with that neighbouring Nation. One might have naturally expected that doctrines so absurd, so nonsensical, and so pernicious, would have been treated with that contempt they deserve, and would have sunk into oblivion. But when one not only finds such tenets held, but Societies of men formed, who meet with the express purpose of disseminating such doctrines, and who hold a regular correspondence with other societies in a neighbouring Nation, it is time for every sober man who is at all interested in the safety and welfare of his Country, as much as in him lies, to endeavour to crush such unconstitutional and pernicious doctrines. ...

Mr Justice Ashhurst's Charge to the Grand Jury for the County of Middlesex... November 19th 1792. Lamoine, [6], pp. 448–9.

DOCUMENT 15 A PAINE BURNING

The following account, written to Jemima, Marchioness Grey, by Joseph Pawsey, the Steward of her property Wrest Park, Bedfordshire, describes a ritual Paine burning which appears to have originated, not from the actions of a Reeves society, but from among the plebeian participants themselves.

17 January 1793

The Effigies of Tom Paine having been Burnt at Wooburn, Bedford, Ampthill etc; I believe put it into the Heads of the Wheelwrights Apprentices and Journeymen and some shoemakers and other Lads in Silsoe to do the same, they carried him round the Vilage, and to Flitton, siting upon an Ass, with his Face to its Tail, and when they Returnd they Hung him and then shot at Him, after afterwards Burnd Him they Beggd round the Vilage and got a five shillings which they Expended in Gun Powder and Beer – the meeting was quite orderly, and without any Riot, the Fire-Arms they had were no other than three or four old Fowling pieces they Borrowd in the Vilage.

Bedfordshire Record Office [hereafter RO], L 30/9/73/10.

DOCUMENT 16 A BOOKSELLER'S APOLOGY

It was not always considered necessary to proceed with a prosecution for seditious libel. A public apology by a bookseller could be accepted by magistrates as sufficient.

Bingley, Nov. 11th., 1793

Whereas I, Jonas Nicholson, of Halifax, Bookseller, have inadvertently and unadvisedly exposed to Sale, and actually sold a certain Printed Paper, which (in the Opinion of the Justices before who an Information has been laid) was printed and published with a seditious intent ... whereby in the Opinion of the said Magistrates, I have rendered myself liable to a criminal Prosecution: and whereas the said Magistrates have humanely recommended all further Proceedings to be stopt, in Consideration of my acknowledging my Misconduct herein, in the public Papers, and promising to be more cautious in future; – Now, I do hereby acknowledging my Error in so doing, and promise faithfully that I will be more circumspect in the future in exposing to Sale any Publications which may tend in any Degree to disturb the public Peace of the Country, or to mislead the minds of the people. ...

Leeds Mercury, 16 November 1793; *Leeds Intelligencer*, 18 November 1793

DOCUMENT 17 WHICH DIRECTION FOR REFORM?, 1794

The following is an extract from a letter from Hardy, as secretary of the LCS, to Daniel Adams, the secretary of the SCI, dated 27 March 1794.

The London Corresponding Society conceives that the moment is arrived when a full and explicit declaration is necessary from all the friends of freedom – Whether the late illegal and unheard of prosecutions and sentences shall determine us to abandon our Cause or shall excite us to pursue a Radical Reform with an ardour proportioned to the Magnitude of the object and with the Zeal as *distinguished* on *our* parts as the *treachery* of others in the Same glorious Cause is *Notorious* – The Society for Constitutional Information is therefore required to determine whether or no they will be ready when called upon to act in Conjunction with *this* and *other societies* to obtain a fair Representation of the PEOPLE – Whether they concur with us in seeing the necessity of a *Speedy Convention* for the purpose of obtaining in a Constitutional and Legal method a redress of those grievances under which we at present labour and which can only be effectually removed by a full and fair Representation of the *People* of Great

Britain – The L. Corresponding Society cannot but remind their friends that the present Crisis demands all the prudence, Unanimity and Vigor, that ever were or can be exerted by *Men and Britons* nor do they doubt but that manly firmness and consistency will finally and they believe *shortly* terminate in the full accomplishment of their wishes.
Thale, [8], p. 125.

DOCUMENT 18 RESPONSES TO THE TREASON TRIAL ACQUITTALS

(a) *The* Sheffield Iris *commenting on Hardy's acquittal.*

We have not unfrequently boasted our peculiar Privileges as Britons. We must now however speak more locally, and boast of our Privileges as *Englishmen.* When we contemplate the fate of Muir and Palmer, and contrast it with the glorious triumph of Hardy, we ought to be peculiarly grateful to Providence, that we are blessed with mild *English* laws, equitable Courts of Justice, and upright, impartial, independent, free-minded *English* Juries, who are an honour to their country and to human nature. How must our Northern Brethren sigh at their inferiority, and weep that they have not *our* Privileges!

Sheffield Iris, 21 November 1794.

(b) *The* Cambridge Intelligencer *commenting on Hardy's acquittal.*

Of the *eighty* warrants which were filled up during the sitting of the *Grand Jury*, for treasonable practices, *fifty-three* were actually signed and ready to be issued on the evening of Mr. HARDY's acquittal, on the supposition that there would have been a verdict of conviction. This is a specimen of the extent to which Crown prosecutions would have been carried and acted upon by implication, had a precedent been established for the *revival* of *constructive* treason.

Cambridge Intelligencer, 22 November 1794.

DOCUMENT 19 THE VOLUNTEERS

(a) Handbill announcing the creation of the North York Yeomanry, 1794.

North Riding of Yorkshire: At a General Meeting of the Nobility, Gentry, Clergy, Freeholders, and others of the Said Riding, held at the COURT-HOUSE in NORTHALLERTON, (pursuant to Advertisement) on THURSDAY, the 12th Day of June, 1794, for the taking into Consideration

Measures necessary to be adopted for the internal Defence of this Kingdom.

RESOLVED – THAT in the present alarming and important Situation of this Country, the Noblemen, Gentlemen, Clergy, and Yeomen of the North Riding of the County of YORK, feel themselves called upon to give the utmost Assistance in their Power (under the Sanction of Parliament) to Strengthen the Means of National Defence against any Attempt of Foreign Invasion, and to assist and support the legal constituted Authorities of the Kingdom, in suppressing any Riot or Tumult which may be excited by seditious and designing Men, with a View to subvert our present happy Constitution, and those Laws, under the Blessing of which, every Description of Men in the Country enjoy equal Protection.

That Troops of Cavalry should be adopted with the Approbation of Government, and Sanction of Parliament, to serve during the War.

To consist of Gentlemen and Yeomen, and such Persons as they shall bring forward, to be approved of by the Lord Lieutenant, under Authority of His Majesty. ...

Ashcroft, [119], p. 21.

(b) Handbill calling for Volunteers, 1798.

CHELMSFORD, 2d APRIL, 1798

It is a serious truth that the people in general of this Commercial Country, can with difficulty be brought to turn their minds seriously on the necessity of forming themselves into Military Corps. Is it possible that any young and active Briton *can at such a period as the present*, think that he is discharging that duty he owes to himself – his Country – his aged Parent – his female Connections and Acquaintance – and to his Posterity, if he at this moment finds himself unattached to some Regiment or Volunteer Corps, panting with a virtuous ardour to distinguish himself in the glorious defence of his Country and its Constitution? Surely there is not an Englishman so base as unresistingly to submit to be a Slave of France: to have Requisitions laid upon his Country, at the pleasure of Military Officers of the Tyrant Directory. Is there an Englishman who does not clearly foresee that, should France succeed, the Youth of Briton will be dragged into their Armies, to extend their destructive and plundering depredations to any part of the globe, that these Tyrants of Europe may think it worth while to spoil?

Gallant Youths of this happy Isle, rouse yourselves from this apparent state of insensibility of your present arduous situation! If you let pass in inactivity the present moment which calls aloud for exertion, it will be too late – in vain will you begin military organisation when once the Enemy have landed: the forming a Company or Regiment fit to meet an Enemy with any hope of success, is not the business of one week, no, nor one month! – Read with a proper impression, of the incapability of the Swiss the other day to resist, from not knowing the use of arms!* – Imitate their prowess, but take warning from their tardiness in preparation.

*The Loyal Inhabitants of this Town, being desirous, in the present critical State of the Country, of forming a *Volunteer Corps*, a Meeting has been convened, by Notice given in the Church, to be held in the Vestry to-morrow, at Twelve o'Clock, for the purpose of taking the measure into consideration.

Essex RO, D/DGg [L/U] 3/2.

(c) Declaration required of all members of the Royston Armed Association, 1798.

[We declare] Our firm attachment to His Majesty King George the Third and to the constitution of this country as by law established which we will use our utmost endeavours to transmit inviolate to posterity. That considering French principles as absurd and French practices detestable we view with surprise and abhorrence any attempts to disseminate the one or to follow the example of the other and that we will resist both to the utmost of our power whether they be insidiously recommended to our imitation by treacherous friends or forcibly obtruded on us by an invading army.

Cookson, [124], p. 25.

DOCUMENT 20 ADVERTISEMENT FOR A QUOTAMAN

WANTED
For the parish of Craike, near Easingwold,
Betwixt and Easter Sunday next [sic]
AN able-bodied single MAN, to
serve in his MAJESTY'S NAVY. – Any
person properly qualified, who may be inclined to
enter, by applying to Edward Lief and Robert
Walker, Churchwardens and Overseers of the
Poor for the said Parish, will receive THIRTY
GUINEAS (or as they agree) as soon as enrolled.

March 31, 1795

York Chronicle, 2 April, 1795.

DOCUMENT 21 JOHN REEVES ON THE CONSTITUTION

John Reeves published his Thoughts on the English Government *as four letters between 1795 and 1800. The sentiments of the following passage, with its downplaying of the role of parliament, led to his prosecution for sedition.*

...Unambitious, and preferring the quiet and peace, which enables them to pursue their own affairs, to the power and splendour of managing those of the public, the English yield a willing obedience to a Government not of their own chusing: it is an Hereditary King, who bears all the burthen of Government, who is endued with all the power necessary to carry it on, and who enjoys all the honour and pre-eminence necessary to give splendour to so high a station. It is the *King's Peace*, under which we enjoy the freedom of our persons and the security of our property: he *makes*, and he *executes* the Laws, which contain the rules by which that peace is kept; and for this purpose, all officers, civil and military, derive their authority from him. Still further to strengthen this all powerful sway, two qualities are added that seem to bring this Royal Sovereignty, as far as mortal institutions can be, still nearer to the Government of Heaven. First, This Power is to have perpetual continuance – *the King never dies.* – Secondly, Such unbounded power shall be presumed to be exercised with an eminent goodness; and it is accordingly held that – *the King can do no wrong*; – meaning that his person is so sacred that wrong shall never be imputed to him.

...a qualification is annexed to the power of the King, first of *making*, and secondly, of *executing*, the Laws: by which his subjects are admitted to participate in a share of those high trusts.

Accordingly, the King can *enact* no Laws without the *advice and consent*, not only of *the Lords Spiritual and Temporal*, who are in some sort counsellors of his own chusing, but also of the *Commons in Parliament assembled. ...*

His power in *executing* the Laws is qualified by joining Grand and Petty Juries, in the administration of Justice, with his Judges. ...

In fine, the Government of England is *a Monarchy*; the Monarch is the antient stock from which have sprung those goodly branches of the Legislature, the Lords and Commons, that at the same time give ornament to the Tree and afford shelter to those who seek protection under it. But these are still only branches, and derive their origin and their nutriment from their common parent; they may be lopped off, and the Tree is a Tree still; shorn indeed of its honours, but not, like them, cast into the fire. The Kingly Government may go on, in all its functions, without Lords and Commons: it has heretofore done so for years together, and in our times it does so during every recess of Parliament; but without the King *his* Parliament is no more.

John Reeves, *Thoughts on the English Government. Addressed to the Quiet and Good Sense of the People of England*, 1795. Claeys, [3], vol. 8, pp. 224–5.

DOCUMENT 22 SPENCE ON THE END OF OPPRESSION

Thomas Spence, a former schoolmaster from Newcastle-upon-Tyne, was active among radicals in London during the 1790s. He urged that reform must begin with a change in the system of landholding since this was the root of all problems. His agrarian ideals and proto-socialism had a marked impact on popular radicalism down to the Chartist period. This pamphlet was written in the popular form of a dialogue, in this instance between an old man and a young man.

O[ld] M[an]. Landed Property always was originally acquired either by conquest or encroachment on the common Property of Mankind. And as those public Robbers did never shew any degree of conscience or moderation in their usurpations, it cannot be expected that the multitudes thus disinherited and enslaved for ages should in the day of reclamation, through an effeminate and foolish tenderness, neglect the precious opportunity of recovering at once the *whole* of their Rights.

Y[oung] M[an]. But I am speaking of the seeming hardships of depriving modern Purchasers of their Property.

O.M. Those modern Purchasers are not ignorant of the manner in which Landed Property was originally obtained, neither are they sorry for it, nor for any imposition by which they can get Revenue. And every one knows that buying stolen Goods is as bad as stealing.

Y.M. You are entirely right. The conduct of our rich Men is not such as to create much respect for their Property. The whole of their study is to create Monopolies and to raise Rents and Revenues; and, like the Grave, their endless cry is, Give! Give!

O.M. And what was originally obtained by the Sword, they determine to detain by the Sword. Are they not and their Minions now in Arms under the name of Yeomanry, Volunteers etc? And what means the inveterate War commenced by the Aristocracy of the World against France? They know that Mankind once enlightened will not brook their lordliness, nor be content with their Rights by peace-meal; therefore they exert every nerve to prevent light from spreading, and the union of the People. ...

Y.M. It is amazing that Paine and other Democrats should level all their Artillery at Kings, without striking like Spence at this root of every abuse and of every grievance.

O.M. The reason is evident: they have no chance of being Kings; but many of them are already, and the rest very foolishly and wickedly hope to be sometime or other landlords, lesser or greater. ...

Thomas Spence, *The End of Oppression*, 1795. Dickinson, [5], pp. 34–5.

DOCUMENT 23 LCS RESOLUTIONS, OCTOBER 1795

The following resolutions were among those presented to, and approved by the crowd at the open-air meeting held by the LCS in a field near Copenhagen House on 26 October 1795.

RESOLVED,

1st. That the present awful and alarming state of the British Empire, demands the serious attention of our fellow countrymen.

2d. That its unexampled distresses call for immediate and effectual redress.

3d. That we are fully persuaded the present exorbitant price of the necessaries of life (notwithstanding the late abundant harvest) is occasioned partly by the present ruinous war; but chiefly by that pernicious system of monopoly, which derives protection from the mutilated and corrupt state of Parliamentary Representation.

4th. That the enormous load of taxes, under which this *almost* ruined country groans, together with its unparalleled National Debt, (which has been greatly encreased by the present war) threatens the British Nation with *total* ruin.

5th. That the inflexible obstinacy of Ministers, in continuing the present cruel, unjust, and disgraceful war – a war which has stained the earth and seas with so much human blood – calls aloud for the execration of every friend of humanity.

6th. That the present Government of France, is as capable of maintaining the *accustomed relations of peace and amity* with the King of Great Britain, as with the Elector of Hanover.

7th. That we remain fully convinced that the permanent peace, welfare and happiness of this Country, can be established only by restoring to our fellow Countrymen their natural and undoubted rights, UNIVERSAL SUFFRAGE and ANNUAL PARLIAMENTS. ...

10th. That we believe the period is not far distant, when Britons must no longer depend upon any party of men for the recovery of their Liberties.

11th. THAT THE ONLY HOPE OF THE PEOPLE IS IN THEMSELVES.

Thale, [8], pp. 316–17.

DOCUMENT 24 LOYALIST ATTACKS ON THELWALL'S LECTURES, 1796

In August and September 1796 John Thelwall travelled to East Anglia to give a series of lectures on Classical History. The following is taken from his account of the loyalist attacks on his six lectures in Yarmouth.

On the first and second nights ... a party was formed, consisting of two or three *Clergymen*, some Officers of the Militia (most of them *disguised* in coloured clothes) a fellow employed to look after the Emigrants, and a hanger-on or two (place expectants) of Government, who attempted to breed disturbance in the Lecture Room, while a parcel of boys without, instigated by a Naval Officer, who offered them five guineas if they would pull down the house, co-operated with the detachment within, by all the noise and uproar they were capable of making. ...

[The third meeting was broken up by about 90 sailors armed with bludgeons and cutlasses, who tried to seize Thelwall.] The first persons who escaped from this long conflict, applied immediately to the mayor, then at the assembly, for assistance to suppress the riot; but instead of being attended to, one of them was threatened himself with commitment, and one of the persons in company with this chief magistrate indecently exclaimed, and met with no rebuke, that 'it served the people right; and as for the damned lecturer, he hoped they would beat him to pieces.'

John Thelwall, *An Appeal to Popular Opinion against Kidnapping and Murder; including a Narrative of the late Atrocious Proceedings at Yarmouth*, London, 1796 (British Library).

DOCUMENT 25 MANIFESTO OF THE FLEET DELEGATES AT THE NORE TO THEIR FELLOW COUNTRYMEN, JUNE 1797

The Manifesto from which the following is extracted was intended to be printed and posted on the Royal Exchange in London. One of the Nore delegates delivered it to an American ship with 3 guineas for the printing costs. It was never printed.

Shall we who have endured the toils of a tedious, disgraceful war, be the victims of tyranny and oppression which vile, gilded, pampered knaves, wallowing in the lap of luxury, choose to load us with? Shall we, who amid the rage and tempest and the war of jarring elements, undaunted climb the unsteady cordage and totter on the topmast's dreadful height, suffer ourselves to be treated worse than the dogs of London Streets? Shall we, who in the battle's sanguinary rage, confound, terrify and subdue your proudest foe, guard your coasts from invasion, your children from slaughter, and your lands from pillage – be the footballs and shuttlecocks of a set of tyrants who derive from us alone their honours, their titles and their fortunes? No, the Age of Reason has at length revolved. Long have we been endeavouring to find ourselves men. We now find ourselves so. We will be treated as such. Far, very far, from us the idea of subverting the government of our beloved country. We have the highest opinion of our Most Gracious Sovereign, and we hope none of those measures taken to deprive us of the common rights of men have been instigated by him.

... Hitherto we have laboured for our sovereign and you. We are now obliged to think for ourselves, for there are many (nay, most of us) in the Fleet who have been prisoners since the commencement of the War, without receiving a single farthing. Have we not a right to complain? Let His Majesty but order us to be paid and the little grievances we have made known redressed, we shall enter with alacrity upon any employment for the defence of our country. ...

PRO Adm. 1/5486.

DOCUMENT 26 SEAMAN'S OATH DURING THE 1798 MUTINIES

The following is a copy of an oath allegedly taken on HMS Defiance *in June 1798.*

I swear to be true to the free and united Irishmen who are now fighting our cause against Tyrants and Oppressors and to defend their Rights to the last Drop of my Blood and to keep all Secret and I do agree to carry the ship into Brest the next time the Ship looks out ahead at sea and to kill any Officer and Man that shall hinder us ... and to hoist a Green Ensign with a Harp in it and afterwards to kill and destroy the Protestants.

PRO Adm. 1/5346.

DOCUMENT 27 THREATENING POSTERS FROM THE FOOD RIOTS

(a) Notice circulated in Sheffield, 4 August 1795, which allegedly was the cause of a violent confrontation between crowds and troops.

Treason! Treason! Treason!
Against the People!

The People's humbugg'd! A Plot is discovered! Pitt and the Committee for

Bread are combined together to starve the Poor into the Army and Navy! and to starve your Widows and Orphans! – God help ye Labourers of the nation! You are held in requisition to fight in a bad Cause! – A Cause that is blasted by Heaven! and damn'd by all good Men!

Every one to his Tent, O *Israel*!

Sharpen your weapons, and spare not! for all the Scrats in the nation are united against your Blood! your Wives and your little ones! – Behold! good Bread at six shillings per stone! – And may every wearer of a Bayonet be struck with Heaven's loudest Thunder, that refuse to help you! – Fear not your Lives! Aristocrats are Scoundrels! Cowards! – Cursed be the Farmers and Promoters of the Corn-Bill! and let all the people say Amen!

York Courant, 17 August 1795.

(b) Notice posted in Bath, March 1800.

Peace
and Large Bread
or
a King without a Head
as we can't make a Riot
We'll do things more quiet
As provisions get higher
The greater the Fire!
Beware
A stitch in time saves nine

PRO H.O. 42.49, enclosed in Ph. George (Deputy Town Clerk of Bath) to the Master of the Rolls, 16 March 1800.

(c) Notice posted in Ramsbury, Wiltshire, on night of 10–11 June 1800.

Dear Brother Britons North and South Younite your selves in one Body and stand true Downe with your Luxzuaras Government both Spirital and temporal or you starve with Hunger they have stript you of bread Chees Meate etc etc etc etc etc. Nay even your Lives have they taken thousands on their expeditions let the Burbon Family defend their owne cause and let us true Britons loock to our selves let us Banish some to Hannover whence they came from Downe with your Contitucion Arect a rebublick or you and your offsprings are to starve the Remainder of our Days dear Brothers will you lay down and die under man eaters and have your offspring under that Burden that Blackgard Government which is now eatan you up.

God save the Poor and down with Gorge III

PRO H.O. 42.50, Enclosed in Edward Merick (Vicar of Ramsbury) to Portland, 12 June 1800.

(d) Notice posted in Windsor, 13 December 1800.

This is to give notice to king G.3. and all his tyrannical crew that we will have bread at 6d. pr. loaf and meat at 4d. pr lb or we the starved poor are determined he shall be shot and the farmers and others that hold their corn from market their ricks and corn shall be burnt for we value not our own lives so as we can get rid of these tyrants.

PRO H.O. 42.55.71, enclosed in Colonel Manningham to John King, 14 December 1800.

DOCUMENT 28 GOVERNMENT ATTITUDES TO THE WAR

The question of the aims of the war against Revolutionary France divided Pitt's ministry from the outset. The following minute, prepared by Henry Dundas on 22 September 1800, sketches these ministerial divisions.

State of the Cabinet.

Some of us are of opinion that the repose of Europe, and the security of Great Britain are only to be obtained by the Restoration of the ancient Royal Family of France, and that every operation of war, and every step to negotiation, which does not keep that object in view, is mischievous, and will ultimately prove to be illusory.

Some of us are of opinion that although we ought not to consider the Restoration of the ancient Royal Family as a *sine qua non*, we ought not to treat with revolutionary Government and that the present Government of France is of that description.

Some of us are of opinion that, whatever has been the foundation of the present Government, it has established within its power, the whole authority, civil and & military of the country and that we are not warranted to reject negotiations with a Government so constituted and *de facto* existing.

Some of us are of opinion, that although we ought to negotiate with the present Rulers of France, we ought only to do it in conjunction with our allies, particularly the Emperor of Germany, it being the interest of this Country, closely to connect our Interest with his.

Some of us are of opinion, that if ever it was practicable to influence by Force of Arms the interior Government of France, that time is past. That it is even problematical if the present revolutionary Principles of that country are not maintained and supported in place of being weakened by the external pressure of its Enemies. That we may lose much, and can gain nothing by implicating our Interests with Austria, and that we have nothing solid to depend upon, except what we may derive from our own vigor and energy, and that under these circumstances, it is our Duty neither to court nor to repudiate negotiation, but when we do enter upon it, to do it not in a spirit of despondency, but with a sense and feeling of Dignity, determined to insist on Terms adequate to our successes, and compatible with the permanent Security of our National Interests.

In this short statement I believe I have given a just analysis of the leading Principles which operate upon the opinion of the Persons who at present compose the confidential Councils of His Majesty. If this difference of sentiment could be considered as so many abstract Theories, it would be of no moment to examine them minutely, but they daily enter into every separate Discussion which occurs on the subject of either Peace or War. It is natural for every man to be partial to his own view of a subject, but neither that partiality, nor the sincere personal respect or reciprocal good opinion we may entertain of each other, can blind us so far as not to perceive that amidst such jarring opinions, the essential Interests of the Country must daily suffer.

It is earnestly hoped that Mr Pitt will take these observations under his serious consideration before it is too late.

British Library, Melville Papers, Additional MSS 40102, ff. 79–81.

DOCUMENT 29 GILLRAY'S CARICATURES

The late eighteenth and early nineteenth centuries were a golden age of caricature in Britain. Among the most celebrated caricaturists was James Gillray. He specialised in political and social subjects, and his works were on view to the public in Hannah Humphrey's print shop window. Gillray attacked politicians on all sides, though during the decade of the French Revolution his political work tended to be rather more critical of the Foxites. The Zenith of French Glory, *published on 12 February 1793, was his perspective on the execution of Louis XVI.* Presages of the Millenium, *published on 4 June 1795, shows Pitt riding over the Foxites with their demands for peace. The portrayal of Pitt, naked, a sword in one hand and famine in the other is far from flattering. The four demonic figures in his horse's tail are, clockwise from the left, Henry Dundas, Lord Kenyon (Lord Chief Justice), Burke, and Lord Loughborough.*

(a) The Zenith of French Glory

Source: British Library, BMC 8300

(b) Presages of the Millenium

Source: British Library, BMC 8655

WHO'S WHO

Addington, Henry (1757–1844) Politician. Entered parliament 1784. Supporter of Pitt. Speaker of the Commons 1789–1801. Prime minister following Pitt's resignation. His government negotiated the Peace of Amiens. Created Viscount Sidmouth in 1805. Lord Privy Seal in the Talents ministry. Home secretary 1812–21.

Binns, John (1772–1854) Political radical. Born Dublin. Moved to London with brother in 1794. Member of LCS and linked with revolutionary groups in England and Ireland. Acquitted of treason (1798). Held under the suspension of the Habeas Corpus Act (1799–1801). Emigrated to USA on release. Became relatively successful newspaper owner and local politician in Philadelphia.

Blake, William (1757–1827) Artist, poet, mystic. Born London, began life as an engraver. Developed own style of intaglio (relief etching) to illustrate his poetry. Enormously productive during the period of the French Revolution, notably with *Songs of Innocence* (1789), *Songs of Experience* (1794), the visionary and prophetic *Book of Thel* (1789–94), and pictures such as *The Elohim creating Adam* and *Newton* (both 1795). On the fringe of radical politics and millenarianism, he was tried and acquitted of treason in 1804.

Bowles, John (1751–1819) Barrister and magistrate. Best known as loyalist pamphleteer during revolutionary and Napoleonic period. Received payment from government for some writings.

Brothers, Richard (1757–1824) Millenarial prophet. Born Newfoundland. Served in Royal Navy as midshipman then lieutenant during American war. Had religious revelation while living in London (1790). Published *A Revealed Knowledge of the Prophesies and Times* (1794) which was read in France and the United States as well as in Britain. Seen by many as a prophet of the millennium. Interrogated by the Privy Council, March 1795, and committed to an asylum as insane. Released in 1806.

Burke, Edmund (1729–97) Politician and political writer. Born Dublin. Read for the bar. Entered parliament 1765, becoming inspirational figure in the Whig Party as orator and author. *Thoughts on the Causes of the Present Discontents* (1770) was influential pamphlet critical of growing royal influence and faction. Sympathetic to American colonists. Key figure in impeachment of Warren Hastings for abuse of power in India. Began to be disillusioned with Whigs during Regency Crisis. Alarmed by French Revolution, and publicly broke with Fox over this.

Camden, John Jeffreys Pratt, 2nd Earl (1759–1840) Politician. Entered parliament 1780. Held minor offices in Pitt's government. Succeeded to father's earldom 1794. Lord Lieutenant of Ireland 1795; unsympathetic to Catholic emancipation and resigned after 1798 rebellion. Served in various minor cabinet posts 1804–12 when created Earl of Brecknock and Marquis of Camden.

Cornwallis, Charles, 1st Marquis (1738–1805) Soldier. Son of 1st Earl Cornwallis. Distinguished military career, though surrender at Yorktown (1781) was final British disaster in American War of Independence. Subsequently served in India, returning in 1793 when created marquis and appointed master general of the ordnance. Lord Lieutenant of Ireland 1798–1801. Helped negotiate Peace of Amiens.

Despard, Col. Edward Marcus (1751–1803) Soldier and revolutionary. Came from Irish gentry family. Distinguished military career serving principally in West Indies. Involved in radical politics from late 1790s. Links with Irish rebels, leading to conspiracy of 1802 for which he was executed.

Dundas, Henry (1742–1811) Politician. Born Scotland. Entered parliament 1774. Held ministerial posts under Pitt, notably home secretary (1791–94), secretary of war (1794–1801), and managed Scottish politics in Pitt's interest. Created Viscount Melville 1802.

Emmet, Robert (1778–1803) Irish patriot. Born Dublin, son of physician to the viceroy. As a student at Trinity College, Dublin, showed sympathy with United Irishmen. Elder brother, Thomas Addis Emmet, was a member of United Irishmen and imprisoned following 1798 rebellion. Travelled in Europe 1800–2, meeting Bonaparte. Executed for role in Dublin rising of 1803.

Erskine, Thomas (1750–1823) Politician and lawyer. Friend of Fox. Best known for skill and eloquence defending Lord George Gordon (1781), Tom Paine (1792), Hardy, Tooke and Thelwall (1794). Created Lord Chancellor and Baron Erskine in 1806.

Fitzgerald, Lord Edward (1763–98) Irish patriot. Son of 1st Duke of Leinster. Joined army 1779 and served in American war. Cashiered for attending revolutionary banquet in Paris (1793). Expelled from Irish parliament for comments about lord lieutenant (1793). Joined United Irishmen 1796 becoming military commander. Arrested 1798; died of wounds in prison.

Fitzwilliam, William Wentworth Fitzwilliam, 2nd Earl (1748–1833) Politician, and one of the wealthiest English noblemen. A Whig who followed Portland into coalition with Pitt. Briefly lord lieutenant of Ireland (1795) where his sympathy for Catholics and reform rapidly led to his recall.

Fox, Charles James (1749–1806) Politician. Entered parliament 1769. Key figure in Whig Party, highly regarded for attractive personality and oratory. Served briefly in government 1770–72 and 1782–83. Led liberal Whig group sympathetic to French Revolution leading to break first with Burke then with Portland and others. Foreign secretary in Talents ministry 1806.

George III (1738–1820) Succeeded grandfather (George II) as king in 1760. Hard-working and conscientious, which occasionally brought him into conflict with ministers, e.g. initial break with Pitt over Catholic emancipation (1801). First attack of madness (1788) led to Whig attempt to establish a regency, and increased his detestation of Fox. Illness became permanent in 1811, and son, George, Prince of Wales, was appointed Regent.

Gillray, James (1757–1815) Caricaturist. Began as a letter engraver. Produced a few caricatures in early 1770s. Style improved after attending Royal Academy school in 1778. He satirised both political and social developments. For most of his career he lodged with Hannah Humphrey, publisher and print-seller, who displayed his work in her shop window – most famously (from April 1797) at 27 St James's Street.

Godwin, William (1756–1836) Political theorist. Dissenting minister but, after moving to London in 1782, increasingly concentrated on his writing and developing his ideas concerning government, morals and society. *The Enquiry Concerning the Principle of Political Justice* was published in 1793; a 'Jacobin' novel, *Caleb Williams, or Things as they Are*, appeared the following year when he also publicly supported those accused of high treason. Married Mary Wollstonecraft in 1797.

Grenville, William Wyndham, Baron (1759–1834) Politician. Entered parliament 1782. Held a variety of posts under Pitt – speaker of the Commons (1789); took charge of government business in the Lords when created a baron (1790); foreign secretary (1791–1801). Formed Talents ministry (1806).

Grey, Charles (1764–1845) Politician. Eldest surviving son of 1st Earl Grey. Entered parliament 1786. Close associate of Fox, and leading figure in Whig Society of the Friends of the People. As Lord Howick served in Talents ministry as first lord of the Admiralty then, on Fox's death, foreign secretary and leader of the Commons. Succeeded to father's title 1807. Prime minister 1830–34, presiding over the Great Reform Act 1832.

Hardy, Thomas (1752–1832) Political radical and reformer. Born Scotland. Moved to London as shoemaker in 1774. Founder member of LCS (1792). Acquitted of treason (1794), but continued on fringes of London radical politics for next 20 years.

Hoche, General Lazare (1768–97) French soldier. Began life as a stable boy. Enlisted in army, rising to rank of corporal by 1789. Distinguished service in the revolutionary armies brought rapid promotion; appointed general 1793. Defeated allied landing and insurrection in western France (1795); commanded invasion force to Ireland, driven back by bad weather (1796). Rival to Bonaparte. Died (probably of consumption) at height of powers.

Humbert, General Jean-Joseph-Amable (1767–1823) French soldier. Began life supplying skins for glove manufacture. Joined army, elected as an officer at beginning of Revolution. Noted for foolhardy bravery. Commanded Franco-Irish expedition of 1798.

Jones, John Gale (1769–1838) Political radical. Practised as, but never fully qualified as, a surgeon. Prominent member of LCS and leading figure in London Debating clubs for 30 years. Convicted of sedition (1797) but not imprisoned; twice imprisoned for radical behaviour in 1810.

Lake, General Gerard (1744–1808) Soldier. Joined Guards as ensign in 1758; distinguished service in campaigns over next 40 years. Commanded troops in Ulster in 1796; led British forces against Irish rebellion in 1798. Appointed to command in India, 1800–7, where fought a succession of successful campaigns. Created viscount on return.

Loughborough, Alexander Wedderburn, Baron (1733–1805) Politician and lawyer. Born Scotland. Entered parliament 1761. Became chief justice of the Court of Common Pleas and a baron in 1780, and acted as a Whig leader in the

Lords. Broke with Fox in 1792 becoming Lord Chancellor under Pitt. Following Pitt's resignation in 1801 left office and created Earl of Rosslyn.

Mackintosh, James (1765–1832) Writer, reformer, and politician. Born Scotland. Unsuccessful career as doctor. Moved to London 1788 where studied law and became successful writer of liberal tracts (notably *Vindiciae Gallicae*). Sympathetic to French Revolution and moved in Foxite circles. Grew to admire Burke and renounced support for Revolution because of its violence. Remained moderate reformer, especially in regard to criminal law. Entered parliament 1813.

Malmesbury, James Harris, Baron (1746–1820) Diplomat. Began career in British embassy in Madrid (1768), subsequently serving with distinction in Prussia, Russia, and the Netherlands. Created baron in 1780. Charged with negotiating with French in 1796 and 1797. Created Earl Malmesbury and Viscount Fitzharris in 1800.

Malthus, Revd Thomas (1766–1834) Demographer and economist. Elected to a fellowship at Jesus College, Cambridge 1793; took holy orders 1797. Best known for his *Essay on the Principle of Population*, published in 1798; in an expanded edition in 1803, and in another four editions over the next 23 years. Professor of modern history and political economy at the East India Company college at Haileybury from 1805 until his death.

Margarot, Maurice (1745–1815) Political radical. Born Devon to foreign parents, educated at University of Geneva. Chairman of LCS (1792). LCS delegate to Edinburgh Convention (1793). Convicted of sedition in Scotland and sentenced to 14 years' transportation. Returned to England from Botany Bay in 1810 and resumed radical activities.

More, Hannah (1745–1833) Religious and moral writer, and philanthropist. Began literary career with pastoral plays during 1760s, but following the death of the actor-manager David Garrick, she turned from the theatre to moral reform and evangelical religion. Best known for the Cheap Repository Tracts (1795–1818). She encouraged Friendly Societies, Sunday Schools, and was greatly involved in philanthropic work with children.

O'Connor, Arthur (1762–1852) Irish patriot. Born Co. Cork. Called to the bar 1788, never practised. Entered Irish parliament 1791. Protestant, but with liberal views and pro–Catholic emancipation. Resigned seat 1795, joined United Irishmen 1796, arrested on charge of seditious libel, February 1797. On release became chief editor of the United Irish paper, *Press*. In England 1798, charged with treason, acquitted but re-arrested on another charge. Liberated 1803. Travelled to France where commissioned in French army. Naturalised Frenchman in 1818.

Paine, Thomas (1737–1809) Political writer. Began working life as a corset maker, then an exciseman. Dismissed from latter post for writing a pamphlet in support of higher pay, he travelled to America in 1774. His pamphlet, *Common Sense* (1776), was the first to call for an immediate declaration of independence and was an enormous success. A series of 11 pamphlets, *The Crisis*, supported the colonists' cause throughout the War of Independence. He returned to England in 1787, and on the outbreak of the French Revolution became involved with radical politics. Charged with seditious libel he fled to France in September 1792. He became a member of the French National Convention, opposed the execution of Louis XVI, was imprisoned and narrowly escaped death during the Terror. He returned from France to America in 1802.

Pitt, William 'the Younger' (1759–1806) Politician. Second son of William Pitt 'the Elder' (Earl of Chatham). Entered parliament 1781; prime minister (1783–1801 and 1804–6). Reorganised nation's finances following American war, but from early 1790s found policies increasingly dictated by need to respond to French Revolution.

Portland, William Henry Cavendish Bentinck, 3rd Duke of (1738–1809) Politician. Titular head of brief Whig government (Fox-North coalition) 1783, and leader of Whigs throughout 1780s. Broke with Fox over French Revolution, entering coalition with Pitt as home secretary in 1794. Prime minister 1807–09.

Price, Dr Richard (1723–91) Moral and political philosopher. Born Wales. Dissenting minister with chapel at Newington Green (north of London) from 1758. Wrote series of pamphlets relating to political economy, and civil and religious liberty. Sympathetic to both American colonists and French Revolution.

Priestley, Dr Joseph (1733–1804) Chemist and reformer. Dissenting minister with strong interest in experimental science. Supporter of Wilkes; sympathetic to American colonists and French Revolution. After falling victim to loyalist riots in 1791 emigrated to America.

Reeves, John (1752–1829) Lawyer and career civil servant appointed, among other roles, as commissioner of bankrupts (1780), clerk to the board of trade (1787), chief justice of the Court of Judicature in Newfoundland (1791), Receiver of Police (1792), King's Printer (1800), joint Superintendent of the Alien Office (1803). Best known for organising the Loyalist Crown and Anchor Association in November 1792 and thereby encouraging the growth of loyalist associations.

Sheridan, Richard Brinsley (1751–1816) Playwright and politician. Born Dublin. He made his name during the 1770s with a series of witty plays. From 1776 he was proprietor and manager of the Drury Lane Theatre. Entered parliament 1780 where he became a close associate of Fox.

Spence, Thomas (1750–1814) Radical political thinker and activist. Born Newcastle upon Tyne. Worked there as a schoolmaster and published plans for a reformed alphabet and an essay critical of existing property divisions, which led to his ejection from the local Philosophical Society. Moved to London (1788), where lived in relative poverty selling pamphlets and drinks from a stall on the corner of Chancery Lane and Holborn. Published much of his own work, including the series *One Pennyworth of Pig's Meat, or Lessons for the Swinish Multitude* (1793–95). Involved with extremists in the LCS. Arrested under the suspension of the Habeas Corpus Act (1798); prosecuted for seditious libel, and sentenced to a year in prison (1801). The Spencean Society was established in 1811 to further his ideas of agrarian reform.

Tandy, James Napper (1740–1803) Irish patriot. Born Dublin; merchant family. Played significant and radical role in the Irish agitation during the American war. Involved with Tone in creation of United Irishmen. Imprisoned for challenging Irish attorney general to duel (1792), after which he left for America. In 1798 sailed to France where he joined troops preparing for invasion of Ireland.

Tate, General William (born? – died?) American/French soldier. Born South Carolina, possibly of Irish parentage. Fought British in American war. Conspired with French agents to 'liberate' Louisiana and the Floridas (1793). Fled to France where enlisted in French army. Commanded French landing in Wales in 1797.

Thelwall, John (1764–1834) Son of London silk mercer. From early age showed preference for poetry, philosophy, and law rather than trade. Publishing essays and verse by late 1780s; also began participating in debating society at Coachmakers' Hall. Made name as a lecturer on radical subjects during early 1790s. Acquitted of treason 1794. Withdrew from politics in 1798 trying, first, farming in Brecon, then establishing himself as a lecturer and teacher of oratory, and developing ways of helping people with a stammer.

Tierney, George (1761–1831) Son of wealthy merchant family. Entered parliament 1789, following disputed election. Lost seat 1790. Re-entered after another disputed election 1796. Active opponent of Pitt, especially on fiscal matters. Made himself prominent by insisting on standing in for Fox following his secession – something not popular with some Foxites, especially aristocrats who looked down on his origins. Held minor government offices under Addington and the Talents ministry.

Tone, Theobald Wolfe (1763–98) Irish patriot. Born Dublin. Barrister. Founder member of the United Irishmen (1791). Following government crackdown on the society, he travelled to America (1795), and then to France (1796) where he negotiated on behalf of the United Irishmen. Captured with a small Franco-Irish invasion force in 1798, he was sentenced to death, but committed suicide in prison.

Tooke, Revd John Horne (1736–1812) Political reformer. His long career in the cause of political reform began with the Wilkes affair in the 1760s. Supported the American colonists, and also, during the 1780s, Pitt. Ran against Fox in the election for Westminster in 1790. Sympathy for French Revolution and involvement with radical politics led to a charge of treason (1794). Acquitted. Elected to parliament 1801, but excluded after one day following an act which rendered persons in holy orders ineligible.

Walker, Thomas (1751–1817) Merchant and political reformer. Born Manchester. Key figure in cotton manufacturers' protest against Pitt's Fustian Tax (1784). Anglican, but supported repeal of Test and Corporation Acts; sympathetic to French Revolution and proposals for parliamentary reform. Falsely charged with treason (reduced to conspiracy) (1794). Acquitted, but broken financially.

Wilberforce, William (1759–1833) Evangelical politician and philanthropist. Born into Hull merchant family. Entered parliament 1780. Religious conversion while travelling in Europe 1795 which led to new direction in career. Remained MP and close friend of Pitt, but became driving force behind series of evangelical reforming campaigns and societies: abolition of the slave trade; British and Foreign Bible Society; London Missionary Society; Society for Bettering the Condition and Increasing the Comforts of the Poor.

Windham, William (1750–1810) Politician. Entered parliament 1784 as a Whig. Alarmed by French Revolution, was one of the first to oppose Fox. Secretary at war in Pitt–Portland coalition. Lost parliamentary seat for opposing Peace of Amiens (1802), but found another. Minister for war in the Talents ministry.

Wollstonecraft, Mary (1759–97) Writer and reformer. Her career reflects the limited opportunities for women at the close of the eighteenth century, beginning by caring for a widow, her mother and her sister, she became a governess. She began writing during the 1780s. In Paris during the Terror she had an unhappy affair resulting in an illegitimate daughter and an attempted suicide. She married William Godwin in 1797, and died following childbirth.

Wyvill, Revd Christopher (1740–1822) Political and religious reformer. A landowner in the East Riding, he is best known for his role in organising the Association Movement of 1780 arguing for economical and parliamentary reform. He continued to support moderate reform during the 1790s, as well as attempts to repeal the Test and Corporation Acts and to abolish the requirement that university students and Anglican priests subscribe to the Thirty-Nine Articles.

BIBLIOGRAPHY

I have divided the bibliography into sections but, as ever, there are books which would easily fit under more than one of the headings. The place of publication is London unless otherwise stated.

PRINTED PRIMARY SOURCES

1 Burke, Edmund, *Reflections on the Revolution in France, 1790* (available in numerous editions).

2 Claeys, Gregory (ed.), *Political Writings of the 1790s*, 8 vols, London/Brookfield, VT: Pickering and Chatto, 1995.

3 Claeys, Gregory (ed.), *The Politics of English Jacobinism: Writings of John Thelwall*, University Park, PA: Pennsylvania State University Press, 1995.

4 Cobban, Alfred (ed.), *The Debate on the French Revolution 1789–1800*, Nicholas Kaye, 1950.

5 Dickinson, H.T. (ed.), *The Political Works of Thomas Spence*, Newcastle-upon-Tyne: Avero, 1982.

6 Lamoine, Georges (ed.), *Charges to the Grand Jury, 1689–1803*, Camden Fourth Series, Vol. 43, Royal Historical Society, 1992.

7 Paine, Thomas, *The Rights of Man, Parts One and Two*, 1791–92 (available in numerous editions).

8 Thale, Mary (ed.), *Selections from the Papers of the London Corresponding Society, 1792–1799*, Cambridge: Cambridge University Press, 1983.

9 Wollstonecraft, Mary, *A Vindication of the Rights of Woman*, 1792 (available in numerous editions).

SECONDARY SOURCES

General surveys and edited collections

10 Brown, P.A., *The French Revolution in English History*, Frank Cass, 1965 (first published, 1918).

11 Bryant, Arthur, *The Years of Endurance 1793–1802*, Collins, 1942.

12 Bryant, Arthur, *The Years of Victory 1802–1812*, Collins, 1944.

13 Christie, Ian R., *Stress and Stability in Late Eighteenth-Century Britain: Reflections on the British Avoidance of Revolution*, Oxford: Clarendon Press, 1984.

14 Clark, Anna, *The Struggle for the Breeches. Gender and the Making of the British Working Class*, Berkeley, CA: University of California Press, 1995.

15 Clark, J.C.D., *English Society, 1688–1832*, Cambridge: Cambridge University Press, 1985 (especially Chapters 4 and 6).

16 Colley, Linda, 'The apotheosis of George III: loyalty, royalty and the British nation, 1760–1820', *Past and Present*, 102 (1984), 94–129.
17 Colley, Linda, 'Whose nation? Class and national consciousness in Britain 1750–1830', *Past and Present*, 113 (1986), 97–117.
18 Colley, Linda, *Britons: Forging the Nation 1707–1837*, New Haven, CT: Yale University Press, 1992.
19 Crossley, Ceri and Small, Ian (eds), *The French Revolution and British Culture*, Oxford: Oxford University Press, 1989.
20 Dickinson, H.T. (ed.), *Britain and the French Revolution*, Basingstoke: Macmillan, 1989.
21 Dickinson, H.T., *The Politics of the People in Eighteenth-Century Britain*, Basingstoke: Macmillan, 1994.
22 Eastwood, David, *Governing Rural England: Tradition and Transformation in Local Government 1780–1840*, Oxford: Clarendon Press, 1994.
23 Emsley, Clive, 'The impact of the French Revolution on British politics', in Crossley and Small (eds) [19], pp. 31–61.
24 Hammond, J.L. and Barbara, *The Village Labourer, 1760–1832*, Longmans, Green and Co., 1911.
25 Hammond, J.L. and Barbara, *The Town Labourer, 1760–1832*, Longmans, Green and Co., 1917.
26 Hammond, J.L. and Barbara, *The Skilled Labourer, 1760–1832*, Longmans, Green and Co., 1919.
27 *History*, 83 (1998) A special edition of the journal (no. 270, April) containing six articles on Pitt and his government.
28 Jarrett, Derek, *The Begetters of Revolution: England's Involvement with France 1759–1789*, Longman, 1973.
29 Jones, Colin (ed.), *Britain and Revolutionary France: Conflict, Subversion and Propaganda*, Exeter: Exeter University Press, Exeter Studies in History, no. 5, 1983.
30 Philp, Mark (ed.), *The French Revolution and British Popular Politics*, Cambridge: Cambridge University Press, 1991.
31 Veitch, G.S., *The Genesis of Parliamentary Reform*, Constable, 1965 (first published, 1913).

Ideas

32 Chase, Malcolm, *The People's Farm: English Radical Agrarianism 1775–1848*, Oxford: Clarendon Press, 1988 (especially Chapter 3).
33 Claeys, Gregory, *Thomas Paine: Social and Political Thought*, Boston/London: Unwin Hyman, 1989.
34 Claeys, Gregory, 'The French Revolution debate and British political thought', *History of Political Thought*, 11 (1990), 59–80.
35 Dickinson, H.T., *Liberty and Property: Political Ideology in Eighteenth-Century Britain*, Weidenfeld and Nicholson, 1977.
36 Dinwiddy, John, 'Interpretations of anti-Jacobinism', in Philp (ed) [30], pp. 38–49.
37 Hampsher-Monk, Iain, 'Civic humanism and parliamentary reform: the case of the Society of the Friends of the People', *Journal of British Studies*, 18 (1979), 70–89.

38 Hampsher-Monk, Iain, 'John Thelwall and the eighteenth-century radical response to political economy', *Historical Journal*, 34 (1991), 1–20.
39 Herzog, Don, *Poisoning the Minds of the Lower Orders*, Princeton NJ: Princeton University Press, 1998.
40 Hole, Robert, 'English sermons and tracts as media of debate on the French Revolution', in Philp (ed.) [30], pp. 18–37.
41 Hole, Robert, *Pulpits, Politics and Public Order in England 1760–1832*, Cambridge: Cambridge University Press, 1989.
42 Kiernan, V.G., 'Evangelicalism and the French Revolution', *Past and Present*, 1 (1952), 44–56.
43 McCalman, Iain, 'Mad Lord George and Madame La Motte: riot and sexuality in the genesis of Burke's *Reflections on the Revolution in France*', *Journal of British Studies*, 35 (1996), 343–67.
44 Schofield, Thomas Philip, 'Conservative political thought in Britain in response to the French Revolution', *Historical Journal*, 29 (1986), 601–22.

Politics and political biography

45 Duffy, Michael, 'The Younger Pitt and the House of Commons', in [27], pp. 217–24.
46 Ehrman, John, *The Younger Pitt*, Vol. 1, *The Years of Acclaim*, 1969; Vol. 2, *The Reluctant Transition*, 1983; vol. 3, *The Consuming Struggle*, 1996, Constable.
47 Harling, Philip, *The Waning of 'Old Corruption': The Politics of Economical Reform in Britain 1779–1846*, Oxford: Clarendon Press, 1996.
48 Mitchell, L.G., *Charles James Fox and the Disintegration of the Whig Party 1782–1794*, Oxford: Clarendon Press, 1971.
49 Mori, Jennifer, 'Responses to revolution: the November Crisis of 1792', *Historical Research*, 69 (1996), 284–305.
50 Mori, Jennifer, *William Pitt and the French Revolution, 1785–1795*, Edinburgh: Keele University Press, 1997.
51 Mori, Jennifer, 'The political theory of William Pitt the Younger', in [27], pp. 234–48.
52 Morris, Marilyn, *The British Monarchy and the French Revolution*, New Haven, CT: Yale University Press, 1998.
53 O'Brien, Patrick, 'Political biography and Pitt the Younger as Chancellor of the Exchequer', in [27], pp. 225–33.
54 O'Gorman, Frank, *The Whig Party and the French Revolution*, Macmillan, 1967.
55 Reid, Loren, *Charles James Fox. A Man for the People*, Longman, 1969.
56 Sack, James J., *From Jacobite to Conservative: Reaction and Orthodoxy in Britain c. 1760–1832*, Cambridge: Cambridge University Press, 1993.
57 Wahrman, Dror, 'Virtual representation: parliamentary reporting and languages of class in the 1790s', *Past and Present*, 136 (1992), 83–113.
58 Wahrman, Dror, *Imagining the Middle Class. The Political Representation of Class in Britain, c. 1780–1840*, Cambridge: Cambridge University Press, 1995.
59 Wilkinson, David, 'The Pitt–Portland Coalition of 1794 and the origins of the "Tory" Party', in [27], pp. 249–64.

60 Ziegler, Philip, *Addington. A Life of Henry Addington, First Viscount Sidmouth*, Collins, 1965.

Radicalism and its repression

61 Cone, Carl B., *The English Jacobins: Reformers in late eighteenth-century England*, New York: Scribner, 1968.
62 Cookson, J.E., *The Friends of Peace: Anti-War Liberalism in England 1793–1815*, Cambridge: Cambridge University Press, 1982.
63 Dickinson, H.T., *British Radicalism and the French Revolution*, Oxford: Blackwell, 1985.
64 Elliott, Marianne, 'The "Despard Conspiracy" reconsidered', *Past and Present*, 75 (1977), 46–61.
65 Emsley, Clive, 'The London "Insurrection" of December 1792: fact, fiction or fantasy?', *Journal of British Studies*, 17 (1978), 66–86.
66 Emsley, Clive, 'An aspect of Pitt's "Terror": prosecutions for sedition during the 1790s', *Social History*, 6 (1981), 155–84.
67 Emsley, Clive, 'Repression, "terror" and the rule of law in England during the decade of the French Revolution', *English Historical Review*, 100 (1985), 801–25.
68 Gill, Conrad, *The Naval Mutinies of 1797*, Manchester: Manchester University Press, 1913.
69 Goodwin, Albert, *The Friends of Liberty: The English Democratic Movement in the Age of the French Revolution*, Hutchinson, 1979.
70 Hone, J. Ann, *For the Cause of Truth: Radicalism in London, 1796–1821*, Oxford: Clarendon Press, 1982.
71 Manwaring, G.E. and Dobrée, Bonamy, *The Floating Republic: An Account of the Mutinies at Spithead and the Nore in 1797*, Geoffrey Bles, 1935.
72 McCalman, Iain, 'Ultra radicalism and convivial debating clubs in London, 1775–1838', *English Historical Review*, 102 (1987), 309–33.
73 McCalman, Iain, *Radical Underworld: Prophets, Revolutionaries and Pornographers in London 1795–1840*, Cambridge: Cambridge University Press, 1988.
74 Orth, John V., *Combination and Conspiracy: A Legal History of Trade Unionism 1721–1906*, Oxford: Clarendon Press, 1991 (especially Chapters 2, 3, and 4).
75 Prochaska, F.K., 'English state trials in the 1790s: a case study', *Journal of British Studies*, 13 (1973), 63–82.
76 Rose, R.B., 'The Priestley Riots', *Past and Present*, 18 (1960), 68–88.
77 Sparrow, Elizabeth, 'The Alien Office, 1796–1806', *Historical Journal*, 33 (1990), 361–84.
78 Thale, Mary, 'London debating societies in the 1790s', *Historical Journal*, 32 (1989), 57–86.
79 Thomis, Malcolm I. and Hunt, Peter, *Threats of Revolution in Britain 1789–1848*, Basingstoke: Macmillan, 1977 (especially Chapter 1).
80 Thompson, E.P., *The Making of the English Working Class*, 2nd edn, Harmondsworth: Penguin, 1968.
81 Thompson, E.P., 'Hunting the Jacobin Fox', *Past and Present*, 142 (1994), 94–140.

82 Wells, Roger, *Insurrection; The British Experience 1795–1803*, Gloucester: Alan Sutton, 1983.
83 Wharam, Alan, *The Treason Trials, 1794*, Leicester: Leicester University Press, 1992.
84 Williams, Gwyn, A., *Artisans and Sans-culottes: Popular Movements in France and Britain during the French Revolution*, 2nd edn, Libris, 1989.

Loyalism

85 Beedell, A.V., 'John Reeves's prosecution for seditious libel 1795–6: a study in political cynicism', *Historical Journal*, 36 (1993), 799–824.
86 Dickinson, H.T., 'Popular conservatism and militant loyalism', in Dickinson (ed.) [20], pp. 103–25.
87 Dozier, Robert R., *For King, Constitution and Country: The English Loyalists and the French Revolution*, Lexington, KY: University Press of Kentucky, 1983.
88 Duffy, Michael, 'William Pitt and the origins of the Loyalist Association movement of 1792', *Historical Journal*, 39 (1996), 943–62.
89 Eastwood, David, 'Patriotism and the English state in the 1790s', in Philp (ed.) [30], pp. 146–68.
90 Ginter, D.E., 'The loyalist association movement of 1792–3 and British public opinion', *Historical Journal*, 9 (1966), 179–90.
91 Mitchell, Austin, 'The association movement of 1792–3', *Historical Journal*, 4 (1961), 56–77.
92 de Montluzin, Emily Lorraine, *The Anti-Jacobins 1798–1800: The Early Contributors to the 'Anti-Jacobin Review'*, Basingstoke: Macmillan, 1988.
93 Pederson, Susan, 'Hannah More meets Simple Simon: tracts, chapbooks, and popular culture in late eighteenth-century England', *Journal of British Studies*, 25 (1986), 84–113.
94 Philp, Mark, 'Vulgar conservatism, 1792–3', *English Historical Review*, 110 (1995), 42–69.
95 Vincent, Emma, ' "The real grounds of the present war": John Bowles and the French revolutionary wars, 1792–1802', *History*, 78 (1993), 393–420.
96 Western, J.R., 'The Volunteer Movement as an anti-revolutionary force', *English Historical Review*, 71 (1956), 603–14.

Regional Studies of Loyalism, Radicalism and Repression

97 Baxter, J.L. and Donnelly, F.K., 'The revolutionary "underground" in the West Riding: myth or reality', *Past and Present*, 64 (1974), 124–32.
98 Booth, Alan, 'Popular loyalism and public violence in the north-west of England, 1790–1800', *Social History*, 8 (1983), 295–313.
99 Dinwiddy, J.R., 'The "Black Lamp" in Yorkshire, 1801–1802', *Past and Present*, 64 (1974), 113–23.
100 Donnelly, F.K. and Baxter, J.L., 'Sheffield and the English revolutionary tradition, 1791–1820', *International Review of Social History*, 20 (1975), 398–423.
101 Jewson, C.B., *The Jacobin City: A Portrait of Norwich and its Reaction to the French Revolution*, Glasgow: Blackie, 1975.

102 Knight, Frida, *The Strange Case of Thomas Walker*, Lawrence and Wishart, 1957.

103 Poole, Steve, 'Pitt's terror reconsidered: Jacobinism and the law in two south-western counties, 1791–1803', *Southern History*, 17 (1995), 65–87.

104 Sellers, Ian, 'William Roscoe: the Roscoe Circle and radical politics in Liverpool 1787–1807', *Transactions of the Historic Society of Lancashire and Cheshire*, 120 (1968), 45–62.

Ireland

105 Curtin, Nancy J., 'The transformation of the Society of United Irishmen into a mass-based revolutionary organisation, 1794–6', *Irish Historical Studies*, 24 (1985), 463–92.

106 Curtin, Nancy J., *The United Irishmen: Popular Politics in Ulster and Dublin 1791–1798*, Oxford: Clarendon Press, 1994.

107 Elliott, Marianne, *Partners in Revolution: The United Irishmen and France*, New Haven, CT: Yale University Press, 1982.

108 Elliott, Marianne, *Wolfe Tone: Prophet of Irish Independence*, New Haven, CT: Yale University Press, 1989.

109 Keogh, Dáire, *'The French Disease': The Catholic Church and Radicalism in Ireland 1790–1800*, Dublin: Four Courts Press, 1993.

110 Pakenham, Thomas, *The Year of Liberty*, Hodder and Stoughton, 1969.

111 Smyth, Jim, *The Men of No Property: Irish Radicals and Popular Politics in the Late Eighteenth Century*, Macmillan, 1992.

112 Wilkinson, David, '"How did they pass the union?": Secret Service expenditure in Ireland, 1799–1804', *History*, 82 (1997), 223–51.

Scotland

113 Brown, David J., 'The government of Scotland under Henry Dundas and William Pitt', in [27], pp. 265–79.

114 Fry, Michael, *The Dundas Despotism*, Edinburgh: Edinburgh University Press, 1992.

115 Logue, Kenneth J., *Popular Disturbances in Scotland 1780–1815*, Edinburgh: John Donald, 1979.

116 Meikle, H.W., *Scotland and the French Revolution*, Glasgow: James Maclehose, 1912.

117 Mullay, Sandy, *Scotland's Forgotten Massacre*, Edinburgh: Moorfoot, 1979.

118 Western, J.R., 'The formation of the Scottish Militia in 1797', *Scottish Historical Review*, 34 (1955), 1–18.

The War

119 Ashcroft, M.Y., *To Escape the Monster's Clutches: Notes and Documents Illustrating the Preparations in North Yorkshire to Repel the Invasion Threatened by the French from 1793*, Northallerton: North Yorkshire County Council, 1977.

120 Blanning, T.C.W., *The Origins of the French Revolutionary Wars*, Longman, 1986.
121 Brewer, John, *The Sinews of Power: War, Money and the English State, 1688–1783*, Unwin Hyman, 1989.
122 Cookson, J.E., *The Friends of Peace: Anti-war Liberalism in England 1793–1815*, Cambridge: Cambridge University Press, 1982.
123 Cookson, J.E., 'The English Volunteer Movement of the French Wars 1793–1815', *Historical Journal*, 32 (1989), 867–91.
124 Cookson, J.E., *The British Armed Nation 1793–1815*, Oxford: Clarendon Press, 1997.
125 Duffy, Michael, *Soldiers, Sugar and Sea Power: The British Expeditions to the West Indies and the War against Revolutionary France*, Oxford: Clarendon Press, 1987.
126 Emsley, Clive, *British Society and the French Wars, 1793–1815*, Basingstoke: Macmillan, 1979.
127 Emsley, Clive, 'The military and popular disorder in England, 1790–1801', *Journal of the Society for Army Historical Research*, 61 (1983), 10–21 and 96–112.
128 Harling, Philip and Mandler, Peter, 'From "fiscal-military" state to laissez-faire state, 1760–1850', *Journal of British Studies*, 32 (1993), 44–70.
129 Mackesy, Piers, *Statesmen at War: The Strategy of Overthrow, 1798–1799*, Longman, 1974.
130 Mackesy, Piers, *War Without Victory: The Downfall of Pitt, 1799–1802*, Oxford: Clarendon Press, 1984.
131 Macleod, Emma Vincent, *A War of Ideas: British Attitudes to the Wars Against Revolutionary France, 1792–1802*, Aldershot: Ashgate, 1998.
132 O'Brien, P.K., 'The impact of the Revolutionary and Napoleonic Wars, 1793–1815, on the long-run growth of the British economy', *Fernand Braudel Center Review*, 12 (1989), 335–95.
133 O'Brien, P.K., 'Public finance in the wars with France, 1793–1815', in Dickinson (ed.) [20], pp. 165–87.
134 Sabine, B.E.V., *A History of Income Tax*, George Allen and Unwin, 1966 (Chapter 2).
135 Schofield, Philip, 'British politicians and French arms: the ideological war of 1793–1795', *History*, 77 (1992), 183–201.
136 Sherwig, John M., *Guineas and Gunpowder: British Foreign Aid in the Wars with France 1793–1815*, Cambridge, MA: Harvard University Press, 1969.
137 Stevenson, John, 'The London "Crimp" Riots of 1794', *International Review of Social History*, 16 (1971), 40–58.
138 Western, J.R., *The English Militia in the Eighteenth Century: The Story of a Political Issue, 1660–1802*, Routledge and Kegan Paul, 1965.

Food shortages and food riots

139 Bohstedt, John, *Riots and Community Politics in England and Wales 1790–1810*, Cambridge, MA: Harvard University Press, 1983.
140 Bohstedt, John, 'Gender, household and community politics: women in English riots, 1790–1810', *Past and Present*, 120 (1988), 88–122.

141 Booth, Alan, 'Food riots in the North-West of England 1790–1801', *Past and Present*, 77 (1977), 84–107.
142 Thompson, E.P., 'The moral economy of the English crowd in the eighteenth century', in E.P. Thompson, *Customs in Common*, Merlin Press, 1991.
143 Thompson, E.P., 'The Moral Economy Reviewed', in E. P. Thompson, *Customs in Common*, Merlin Press, 1991.
144 Wells, Roger A.E., *Dearth and Distress in Yorkshire 1793–1802*, York: University of York, Borthwick Papers No. 52, 1977.
145 Wells, Roger A.E., 'The revolt of the south-west, 1800–1808: a study in English popular protest', *Social History*, 6 (1977), 713–44.
146 Wells, Roger, *Wretched Faces: Famine in Wartime England 1793–1803*, Gloucester: Alan Sutton, 1988.

Art and Literature

147 Bindman, David, *The Shadow of the Guillotine: Britain and the French Revolution*, British Museum Publications, 1989.
148 Butler, Marilyn, *Romantics, Rebels and Reactionaries. English Literature and its Background, 1796–1830*, Oxford: Oxford University Press, 1981.
149 Grenby, M.O., 'The Anti-Jacobin novel: British fiction, British conservatism and the revolution in France', *History*, 83 (1998), 445–71.
150 Hill, Draper, *Mr. Gillray: The Caricaturist*, Phaidon, 1965.
151 Kelly, Gary, *The English Jacobin Novel 1780–1805*, Oxford: Clarendon Press, 1976.
152 Mee, Jon, *Dangerous Enthusiasm: William Blake and the Culture of Radicalism in the 1790s*, Oxford: Clarendon Press, 1992.
153 Scott, Iain Robertson, ' "Things as they are": the literary response to the French revolution 1789–1815', in Dickinson (ed.) [20], pp. 229–49.
154 Thompson, E. P., *Witness against the Beast. William Blake and the Moral Law*, Cambridge: Cambridge University Press, 1993.
155 Thompson, E.P., *The Romantics. England in a Revolutionary Age*, Woodbridge: Merlin, 1997.

INDEX

SEMINAR STUDIES IN HISTORY

General Editors: Clive Emsley & Gordon Martel

The series was founded by Patrick Richardson in 1966. Between 1980 and 1996 Roger Lockyer edited the series before handing over to Clive Emsley (Professor of History at the Open University) and Gordon Martel (Professor of International History at the University of Northern British Columbia, Canada and Senior Research Fellow at De Montfort University).

MEDIEVAL ENGLAND

The Pre-Reformation Church in England 1400–1530 (Second edition)
Christopher Harper-Bill 0 582 28989 0

Lancastrians and Yorkists: The Wars of the Roses
David R Cook 0 582 35384 X

TUDOR ENGLAND

Henry VII (Third edition)
Roger Lockyer & Andrew Thrush 0 582 20912 9

Henry VIII (Second edition)
M D Palmer 0 582 35437 4

Tudor Rebellions (Fourth edition)
Anthony Fletcher & Diarmaid MacCulloch 0 582 28990 4

The Reign of Mary I (Second edition)
Robert Tittler 0 582 06107 5

Early Tudor Parliaments 1485–1558
Michael A R Graves 0 582 03497 3

The English Reformation 1530–1570
W J Sheils 0 582 35398 X

Elizabethan Parliaments 1559–1601 (Second edition)
Michael A R Graves 0 582 29196 8

England and Europe 1485–1603 (Second edition)
Susan Doran 0 582 28991 2

The Church of England 1570–1640
Andrew Foster 0 582 35574 5

STUART BRITAIN

Social Change and Continuity: England 1550–1750 (Second edition)
Barry Coward 0 582 29442 8

James I (Second edition)
S J Houston 0 582 20911 0

The English Civil War 1640–1649
Martyn Bennett 0 582 35392 0

Charles I, 1625–1640
Brian Quintrell 0 582 00354 7

The English Republic 1649–1660 (Second edition)
Toby Barnard 0 582 08003 7

Radical Puritans in England 1550–1660
R J Acheson 0 582 35515 X

The Restoration and the England of Charles II (Second edition)
John Miller 0 582 29223 9

The Glorious Revolution (Second edition)
John Miller 0 582 29222 0

EARLY MODERN EUROPE

The Renaissance (Second edition)
Alison Brown 0 582 30781 3

The Emperor Charles V
Martyn Rady 0 582 35475 7

French Renaissance Monarchy: Francis I and Henry II (Second edition)
Robert Knecht 0 582 28707 3

The Protestant Reformation in Europe
Andrew Johnston 0 582 07020 1

The French Wars of Religion 1559–1598 (Second edition)
Robert Knecht 0 582 28533 X

Phillip II
Geoffrey Woodward 0 582 07232 8

The Thirty Years' War
Peter Limm 0 582 35373 4

Louis XIV
Peter Campbell 0 582 01770 X

Spain in the Seventeenth Century
Graham Darby 0 582 07234 4

Peter the Great
William Marshall 0 582 00355 5

EUROPE 1789–1918

Britain and the French Revolution
Clive Emsley 0 582 36961 4

Revolution and Terror in France 1789–1795 (Second edition)
D G Wright 0 582 00379 2

Napoleon and Europe
D G Wright 0 582 35457 9

Nineteenth-Century Russia: Opposition to Autocracy
Derek Offord 0 582 35767 5

The Constitutional Monarchy in France 1814–48
Pamela Pilbeam 0 582 31210 8

The 1848 Revolutions (Second edition)
Peter Jones 0 582 06106 7

The Italian Risorgimento
M Clark 0 582 00353 9

Bismark & Germany 1862–1890 (Second edition)
D G Williamson 0 582 29321 9

Imperial Germany 1890–1918
Ian Porter, Ian Armour and Roger Lockyer 0 582 03496 5

The Dissolution of the Austro-Hungarian Empire 1867–1918 (Second edition)
John W Mason 0 582 29466 5

Second Empire and Commune: France 1848–1871 (Second edition)
William H C Smith 0 582 28705 7

France 1870–1914 (Second edition)
Robert Gildea 0 582 29221 2

The Scramble for Africa (Second edition)
M E Chamberlain 0 582 36881 2

Late Imperial Russia 1890–1917
John F Hutchinson 0 582 32721 0

The First World War
Stuart Robson 0 582 31556 5

EUROPE SINCE 1918

The Russian Revolution (Second edition)
Anthony Wood 0 582 35559 1

Lenin's Revolution: Russia, 1917–1921
David Marples 0 582 31917 X

Stalin and Stalinism (Second edition)
Martin McCauley 0 582 27658 6

The Weimar Republic (Second edition)
John Hiden 0 582 28706 5

The Inter-War Crisis 1919–1939
Richard Overy 0 582 35379 3

Fascism and the Right in Europe, 1919–1945
Martin Blinkhorn 0 582 07021 X

Spain's Civil War (Second edition)
Harry Browne 0 582 28988 2

The Third Reich (Second edition)
D G Williamson 0 582 20914 5

The Origins of the Second World War (Second edition)
R J Overy 0 582 29085 6

The Second World War in Europe
Paul MacKenzie 0 582 32692 3

Anti-Semitism before the Holocaust
Albert S Lindemann 0 582 36964 9

The Holocaust: The Third Reich and the Jews
David Engel 0 582 32720 2

Britain and Europe since 1945
Alex May 0 582 30778 3

Eastern Europe 1945–1969: From Stalinism to Stagnation
Ben Fowkes 0 582 32693 1

The Khrushchev Era, 1953–1964
Martin McCauley 0 582 27776 0

NINETEENTH-CENTURY BRITAIN

Britain before the Reform Acts: Politics and Society 1815–1832
Eric J Evans 0 582 00265 6

Parliamentary Reform in Britain c. 1770–1918
Eric J Evans 0 582 29467 3

Democracy and Reform 1815–1885
D G Wright 0 582 31400 3

Poverty and Poor Law Reform in Nineteenth-Century Britain, 1834–1914:
From Chadwick to Booth
David Englander 0 582 31554 9

The Birth of Industrial Britain: Economic Change, 1750–1850
Kenneth Morgan 0 582 29833 4

Chartism (Third edition)
Edward Royle 0 582 29080 5

Peel and the Conservative Party 1830–1850
Paul Adelman 0 582 35557 5

Gladstone, Disraeli and later Victorian Politics (Third edition) *Paul Adelman*	0 582 29322 7
Britain and Ireland: From Home Rule to Independence *Jeremy Smith*	0 582 30193 9

TWENTIETH-CENTURY BRITAIN

The Rise of the Labour Party 1880–1945 (Third edition) *Paul Adelman*	0 582 29210 7
The Conservative Party and British Politics 1902–1951 *Stuart Ball*	0 582 08002 9
The Decline of the Liberal Party 1910–1931 (Second edition) *Paul Adelman*	0 582 27733 7
The British Women's Suffrage Campaign 1866–1928 *Harold L Smith*	0 582 29811 3
War & Society in Britain 1899–1948 *Rex Pope*	0 582 03531 7
The British Economy since 1914: A Study in Decline? *Rex Pope*	0 582 30194 7
Unemployment in Britain between the Wars *Stephen Constantine*	0 582 35232 0
The Attlee Governments 1945–1951 *Kevin Jefferys*	0 582 06105 9
The Conservative Governments 1951–1964 *Andrew Boxer*	0 582 20913 7
Britain under Thatcher *Anthony Seldon and Daniel Collings*	0 582 31714 2

INTERNATIONAL HISTORY

The Eastern Question 1774–1923 (Second edition) *A L Macfie*	0 582 29195 X
The Origins of the First World War (Second edition) *Gordon Martel*	0 582 28697 2
The United States and the First World War *Jennifer D Keene*	0 582 35620 2
Anti-Semitism before the Holocaust *Albert S Lindemann*	0 582 36964 9
The Origins of the Cold War, 1941–1949 (Second edition) *Martin McCauley*	0 582 27659 4
Russia, America and the Cold War, 1949–1991 *Martin McCauley*	0 582 27936 4

The Arab–Israeli Conflict
Kirsten E Schulze 0 582 31646 4

The United Nations since 1945: Peacekeeping and the Cold War
Norrie MacQueen 0 582 35673 3

Decolonisation: The British Experience since 1945
Nicholas J White 0 582 29087 2

The Vietnam War
Mitchell Hall 0 582 32859 4

WORLD HISTORY

China in Transformation 1900–1949
Colin Mackerras 0 582 31209 4

US HISTORY

America in the Progressive Era, 1890–1914
Lewis L Gould 0 582 35671 7

The United States and the First World War
Jennifer D Keene 0 582 35620 2

The Truman Years, 1945–1953
Mark S Byrnes 0 582 32904 3

The Vietnam War
Mitchell Hall 0 582 32859 4

272